decorating ideas

QUICK, EASY PROJECTS AND PRACTICAL INSPIRATIONS TO TRANSFORM YOUR HOME IN HOURS

decorating ideas

QUICK, EASY PROJECTS AND PRACTICAL INSPIRATIONS TO TRANSFORM YOUR HOME IN HOURS

stewart and sally walton

HERMES
HOUSE

This edition published by Hermes House
27 West 20th Street, New York, NY 10011

HERMES HOUSE books are available for bulk purchase for sales promotion
and for premium use. For details, write or call the sales director,
Hermes House, 27 West 20th Street, New York, NY 10011;
(800) 354-9657

Hermes House is an imprint of
Anness Publishing Inc.

ISBN 1 84309 709 5

Publisher: Joanna Lorenz
Senior Editor: Clare Nicholson
Photographer: Graham Rae
Stylist: Catherine Tully
Designer: Caroline Reeves

Printed and bound in China

CONTENTS

INTRODUCTION

DECORATION, COLOR, AND DESIGN—never have they been more important than in the modern home as the twenty-first century approaches. Yet, while everyone wants a beautiful home, our lives are busier than ever, and fewer and fewer people have the time or money to devote to intricate decorative schemes.

This book is an ideal starting point for anyone who is looking for ideas to brighten the home and add those individual touches that distinguish the exceptional from the ordinary. In it you will find decorative ideas for every room in the house, from living and dining rooms, to the kitchen—the most important room in the house—to studies, hallways and dens, so often neglected, and then on to children's rooms, bedrooms and bathrooms. Children's rooms, particularly, are very important, and the right decorative details can make a room cool enough for even the most selective teenager. As is so often the case it is a willingness to devote time to the small touches that makes all the difference; effort and imagination are all it takes to brighten your home.

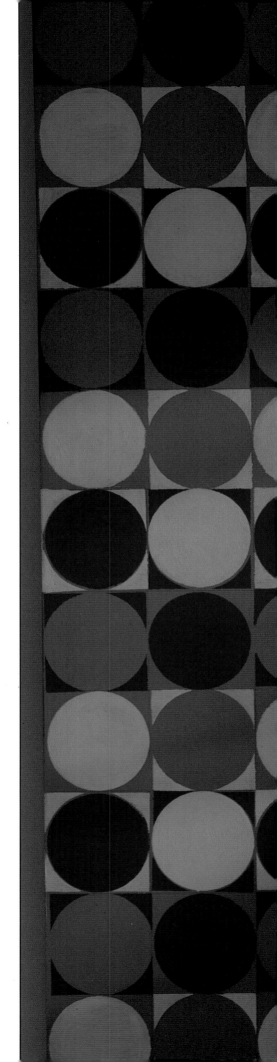

One of the easiest ways to change the look of a room is by making new lampshades. Interesting wall treatments are also a good idea as they are often quick and economical.

LIVING AND DINING ROOMS

IMAGINE A ROOM FULL of light with cool, bleached tones and welcoming textures. Imagine it with bold strokes of color, imaginative details and a hint of elegant understatement. Think beach house, vacations, friends: relaxed, informal, calming. Now imagine this vision of cool as your own living or dining room.

An impossible, or impossibly expensive, dream? Not so. Transforming your living or dining room doesn't mean committing yourself to sweeping changes. Or paying a bevy of professionals to take care of everything from the light bulbs down. It doesn't mean discarding all your favorite things. It does mean using what you already have and concentrating on the details.

Details are important, and in this chapter we look at ways in which an imaginative approach and quality execution can have an effect nothing short of miraculous. We have lots of ideas for both small and larger scale projects to point you in the right direction and tons of tips and shortcuts that can bring even the most professional-looking living/dining room decorating solutions well within anyone's reach.

Disguising a tired old lamp or adding your own unique touches to unadorned cushions sound like minor changes, but when done imaginatively as part of a grand plan the effects can be stunning.

A modern laced chair provides a singular touch that will brighten any room in the house. Covers such as this can be changed to suit the room.

Also, tackling bigger jobs is easier than ever these days. You can turn uninspiring or even damaged walls or floor surfaces into works of art. Strips of wood, painted and then attached at regular intervals to a wall, add interest out of all proportion to the materials used and the skill needed.

Fledgling decorators can even make grand statements with upholstery and curtains—usually mentioned in the same breath as being both expensive and difficult to incorporate successfully—thanks to the staple gun and iron-on hemming. These days you don't even have to sew.

That uplifting new living or dining room is just around the corner.

SUPER SOFA

TRIM A PERFECTLY PLAIN sofa using only a strand of rope that curves gently down the edge of the arm and across the base. This type of decoration works extremely well in a white-on-white color scheme because the eye is aware of the shape, but the embellishment doesn't jump out at you. Other types of trimming that could be used to add a stylish personal touch to your sofa are raffia edging, linen tassels and fringing.

YOU WILL NEED

graph or plain paper

pencil

rope, the length of the area to be trimmed

clear tape

scissors

dressmaker's pins

needle

strong sewing thread

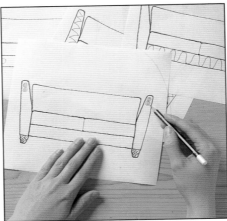

one *Try different designs for the rope on paper, to see what works best; this style seemed to go well with the shape of the arm of the sofa and the lines of the seat.*

two *Bind clear tape around the ends of the rope so that the ends do not fray once the rope is in position.*

three *Cut as close to the end of the tape as you can so that as little is left as possible, but it still holds the rope firmly. Pin the rope onto the sofa and hand-stitch in place.*

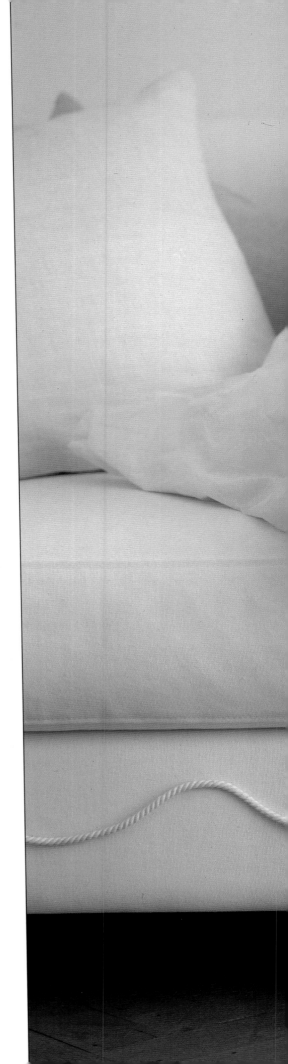

CREAM TOPPING

MAKE A GRAND STATEMENT at the window by creating a valance with a curved edge trimmed with rope. The gentle wave of the valance gives a very gracious, elegant appearance to the treatment, which could, if desired, be echoed in the edging of a loose cover on a chair or sofa. Another wonderful idea is to continue the valance right around the top of the room, so it acts as a wavy trim to the whole area. In this case make sure the valance is the same color as the ceiling so the contrast doesn't jar the eye. Valances can be any shape or size; experiment with pointed V's with bells on, castellations and other variations. Cut the shape out of paper first, and pin it above the curtains to see what effect it will have upon the window and the room as a whole.

YOU WILL NEED

tape measure

2 plates

paper, for template

pencil

valance fabric

dressmaker's scissors

interfacing

dressmaker's pins

needle and basting thread

sewing machine

matching sewing thread

iron

rope

thin strip of wood

hammer and nails or Velcro

one *Measure the window and decide on the dimensions of the valance. Allow an extra 2 inches to attach to the strip of wood. Use plates to make a template.*

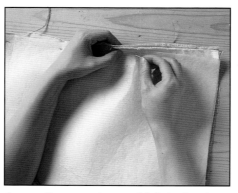

two *Cut two pieces of fabric for the back and the front of the valance. Cut out interfacing to stiffen the valance, and pin the three layers together with right sides facing.*

three *Draw around the template onto the valance piece with a pencil. Pin the fabric just inside the outline.*

four *Cut out the scallops about ½ inch from the outline. Baste along the edge, then machine-stitch.*

five *Trim the interfacing and clip the seam allowance so that the curves will lie flat when turned right side out.*

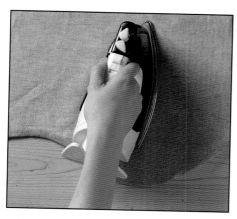

six *Turn the valance right side out and press the scalloped edge. Turn under the straight edge of the valance, then pin and machine-stitch.*

seven *Measure the scalloped edge, and cut a length of rope to fit. Experiment with design options for the rope; for example, you could use two different colors and weights of rope.*

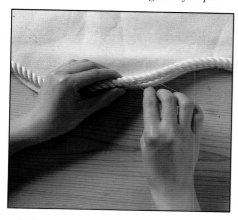

eight *Pin the rope to the valance and hand-sew it in place. To attach the valance to the wall, use a thin strip of wood and nail the valance to it; alternatively, use Velcro to make the valance easy to remove.*

STRING-BOUND LAMP BASE

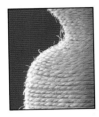

STRING-BINDING IS AN INNOVATIVE way to disguise an unappealing lamp base or to dress up a cheap flea market find. Look for a lamp base with good proportions and a pleasing shape. There are many kinds of string to choose from, ranging from smooth, fine, waxy and white to fat, loose-weave brown twine, and all give different effects. You can paint the string afterward if you want it to fit in with a room's color scheme.

YOU WILL NEED

glue gun with all-purpose glue sticks

china, glass or wooden lamp base

ball of string

scalpel or scissors

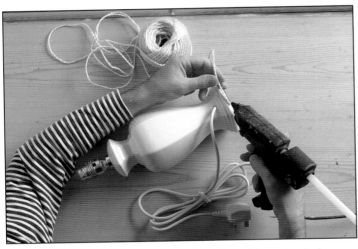

one *Heat the glue gun and apply a dot of hot glue below the flex on the bottom edge of the lamp base. Press the string in place. Apply a thin line of glue to the string and wind it around the lamp base, keeping the string taut as you wind.*

two *Wind the string up around the base, dotting it with glue in key positions to hold the rows tightly together. When you reach the flex, cut the string. Apply a dot of glue on the other side of the hole and start the winding again with a new piece of string.*

three *Apply the glue at intervals as you wind and glue. Use plenty of glue when winding around concave shapes, as this is where the string may sag if it is not held firmly enough.*

four *At the top of the lamp base, apply an extra dot of glue and cut the string at an angle so that it lies flat.*

CLOTH SHADE

LOOSELY WOVEN COTTON, such as that used to make dishcloths, is the ideal fabric for this rustic lampshade. In this project, the fabric is used to cover an ordinary lampshade frame. The tube is opened out and pulled down over the bare lampshade frame. A second layer of fabric then covers the first and is attached so that the edges roll over to create an interesting pattern. Finally a third layer of fabric is pulled over to strengthen and protect the design.

YOU WILL NEED

lampshade frame
tape measure
scissors
1½ yards loosely woven cotton
dressmaker's pins
needle
matching cotton thread
embroidery needle
yellow embroidery floss

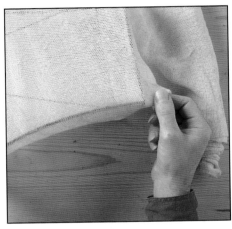

one *Cut a length of cloth three times the height of the frame. Pull the cloth down over the frame so that you have just enough to roll under the bottom.*

two *Divide the remaining cloth in two, then pull a second length down over the frame. Catch the middle of each side along the top and bottom of the frame and pin. The unpinned edges will roll up. Sew the first layer and the pinned section of the second layer securely to the frame.*

three *Pull the third length of cloth down over the frame and pin all around the top and bottom edges. Then stitch to secure the cloth in place.*

four *Cross-stitch around the top and bottom of the shade with a length of yellow embroidery floss to add a subtle finishing touch of color to the shade.*

Curving Rope Design

A PATTERN IN ROPE makes a simple, textured wall finish, perfectly in keeping with today's trend for natural materials in interiors. Rope makes good curves, so the design can be as twisting as you like. For a small area or to make a focal point in a room, mark out squares and put a different, simple design in each square. You could also use the rope to create borders or frames within a room at chair-rail and picture-rail height for posters or paintings.

YOU WILL NEED

scrap paper

pencil

level

straightedge

rope

glue gun and glue sticks or strong adhesive

masking tape

craft knife

white latex paint

paintbrush

one *Plan and draw your design to scale on paper.*

two *Transfer your design to the wall using a level and a straightedge.*

three *Use a glue gun or other suitable adhesive to attach the rope to the wall. Use paint cans or other round objects to help you to make smooth curves. It is easier to cut through the tape if you wrap masking tape around it.*

four *Paint over the wall and rope with white latex paint; you may need a few coats to get an even finish.*

LIFE'S LITTLE LUXURIES

CUSHIONS ARE THE PERFECT way to add a certain style, as well as an element of comfort, to any room. Here, the choice of natural tones and fabrics perfectly complements the simplicity of the sofa. Interest was added to the restrained look with decorative ties, looped buttons and a simple rope trim. If you want a change from the neutral color scheme shown here, add splashes of vibrant color with blues, reds, oranges and purples. Alternatively, blue and white always look fresh and pretty.

YOU WILL NEED

ROPE-TRIMMED CUSHION
about 2 yards fine-gauge rope
dressmaker's pins
plain linen cushion cover
needle
matching sewing thread
cushion pad

CUSHION WITH TIES
cushion pad
tape measure
cotton canvas
dressmaker's scissors
dressmaker's pins
needle
basting thread
iron
sewing machine
matching sewing thread

LOOP AND BUTTON CUSHION
cushion pad
1 yard linen
dressmaker's scissors
dressmaker's pins
needle
basting thread
sewing machine
matching sewing thread
small safety pin
iron
8–10 small buttons

one *For the rope-trimmed cushion cover, use a fine-gauge rope to experiment with different designs. When you are happy with the result, pin the rope onto the cover. Hand-stitch the rope to the cover, neatly finishing off the ends. Insert the cushion pad.*

two *For the cushion with ties, measure the cushion pad and cut one piece of cotton canvas the depth of the cushion plus ⅝ inch all around for seams, and a second piece twice the length plus 6½ inches for turning. Pin, baste, press and sew the seams on the wrong side. Turn it right side out.*

three *For the ties, cut six pieces of cotton canvas 2¼ x 11 inches. Fold each in half lengthwise with wrong sides together and pin, baste, press and machine-stitch a ½-inch seam around two sides. Clip the seams and corners. Turn the ties right side out and slip-stitch the ends closed. Position the ties in pairs and topstitch securely.*

four *For the cushion with loops and buttons, measure the width and length of the cushion pad. Double the length and add 4 inches for the flap opening, plus 1¼ inches for seams all around. You will also need to cut a 3-inch wide strip, the depth of the cushion plus seams. Cut the linen to this size and fold it in half.*

five *To make the piping for the button loops cut a length of linen about 1 inch wide, on the cross. With wrong sides together, pin, baste and machine-stitch the fabric. Trim close to the stitching and, using a small safety pin, turn through to the right side. Press flat.*

six *Measure the buttons and cut the loops to the correct size. Turn over the seam allowance on the cover, then pin and baste the loops in position. Pin, baste and sew the interfacing strip for the back opening on the edge of the cover with the loops.*

seven *With the right sides together, sew a seam all around the cushion cover. Turn it right side out and press. Mark the positions of the buttons with pins, and hand-sew them in place. Insert the cushion pad.*

LIME-WASHED LAMP BASE

ONE OF THE MOST effective ways of updating a dull lamp is to give the base a fashionable paint finish and add a fresh new shade. Look for second-hand bargains at flea markets or antique stores, then give them new life with a special paint treatment. This turned-wood lamp base has been given a limed look by applying and rubbing back two colors. The first, blue-gray coat of paint is rubbed off but remains in the grain and the grooves. The second coat of white paint is also rubbed back, leaving a transparent, lime-washed look.

YOU WILL NEED

plain turned-wood lamp base

fine-grade sandpaper

latex paint: blue-gray and white

paintbrushes

2 cloths

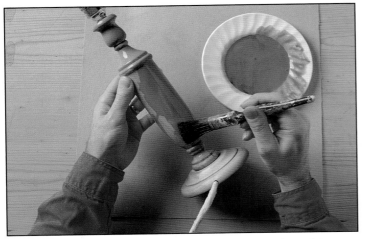

one *Remove any surface finish on the base and sand it to a smooth finish. Then paint the bare wood with a coat of blue-gray paint.*

two *Before the paint has dried, rub it off with a cloth, leaving some color in the grooves and grain. Let dry.*

three *Gently rub the decorative, raised parts of the lamp base with fine-grade sandpaper.*

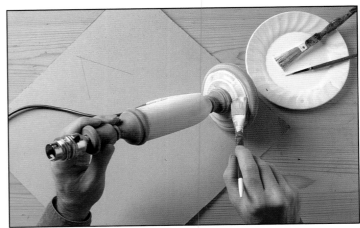

four *Paint the whole lamp base with white latex. Rub off the paint before it has dried, using another cloth, and then let dry. Gently sand the decorative raised parts to create the lime-washed look.*

COLORED STRIPS OF WOOD

SOMETIMES THE SIMPLEST IDEAS are the most effective. Strips of wood spaced on the wall at regular intervals can create an unusual and very dramatic look. Use them on a single wall or in smaller areas, such as the back of an alcove. The key is to keep the colors either tones of the same shade or very contrasting and bold. If time permits, paint the top and bottom of the wood in slightly different shades of the same color to add extra interest. The strips of wood used here are 2 x 1 inch.

YOU WILL NEED

tape measure

wood strips

pencil

saw

matte latex paint:
blue and white

paintbrush

level

drill, with masonry and
wood bits

wall plugs

wood screws

ruler

one *Measure the height and width of the wall to make sure you will have equal spacing all the way up the wall. Cut the wood strips to the required length. Paint the wood strips; you could paint all three sides that will show in different colors, for a more interesting look, or in tones of the same shade, for subtlety.*

two *Use a level to mark a guideline for the first strip, to make sure the wood is absolutely level.*

three *Drill holes in the wall and insert wall plugs. Drill holes in the wood and then screw the strip in place. Mark out the position for the next wood strip; the space between strips must be absolutely even to create the right effect.*

COLOR-WASHED PARQUET

HERRINGBONE PATTERNS ON FLOORS give instant classical elegance, suggestive of the wonderful dark oak parquet floors found in large old houses. However, a fresher look is often wanted, yet with all the interest of the old floors; the introduction of a pale, soft color lifts gloomy dark wood into the realms of light Atlantic beach houses or modern Swedish homes. To keep the interest of the grain of the wood running in different directions, paint each individual piece separately.

YOU WILL NEED

marine-plywood, cut into manageable lengths

miter saw

tape measure

sandpaper

matte latex paint: cream, blue and white

paintbrushes

matte water-based glaze

lint-free cloth

floor adhesive

matte varnish

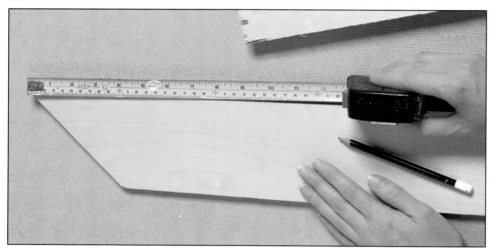

one *Make sure the floor is clean, dry and level. Miter the edges of the marine-plywood strips, using a miter saw. Remember that you must have left- and right-hand miters in equal numbers. Measure your required length for the herringbone pattern and cut as many as you need for the floor.*

two *Smooth any rough edges with sandpaper. Undercoat all the boards with cream matte latex and let them dry completely.*

three *Mix up at least four variations of blue with a very slight tonal difference between them. Add a little matte water-based glaze to each, to delay the drying time. Thin one of the colors with water to make it even more translucent. Paint equal numbers of the boards in each color.*

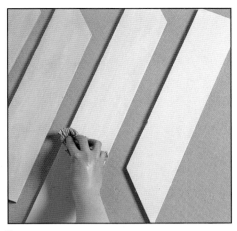

four *With the lint-free cloth, wipe off most of the paint randomly while it is still wet, so that the undercoat shows through. Wipe in the direction of the grain of the wood.*

five *For an even more weathered look, sand some areas of some boards when the paint is dry; this will give contrast when the floor is down. Lay the floor following the instructions for the Parquet project. Finally, ensure that the floor is dry and dust-free, then seal the whole floor with at least two coats of matte varnish.*

GEOMETRIC WALL-BOARD

YOU DO NOT NEED to be an artist to make a work of art for your wall and even make sure it's the right size and in complementary colors for the room. With a piece of fiberboard, a simple, repetitive design and a little time and patience, you can create a wall decoration at very little cost. A stencil is all that's needed and, if you stick to a design made of simple squares and circles, it is no problem to create your own stencil. Alternatively, it is worth looking at the commercial stencils available. There are so many designs to choose from, you are certain to find one you like.

YOU WILL NEED

scrap paper

pencil

ruler

medium-density fiberboard

tape measure

saw

latex paint: blue, yellow and red

paintbrushes

compass

sheet of acetate

craft knife

self-healing cutting mat

masking tape

stencil brush

small artist's brush

rubber

clear varnish

varnish brush

screw eyelets

picture-hanging wire

picture hook

hammer

drill, with masonry and wood bits (optional)

plastic anchors (optional)

wood screws (optional)

one *Choose your colors. You may consider complementing your existing furnishings. Plan out the whole design to scale on paper. Here, a wrapping paper design was used for inspiration.*

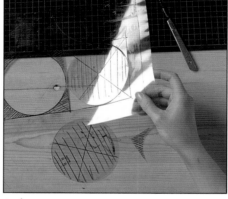

two *Cut the fiberboard to size, apply the blue base coat and let dry. Draw a grid of squares on the painted fiberboard. Use a ruler and compass to draw the stencil on the sheet of acetate. Cut out the stencil carefully using the craft knife on a cutting mat.*

three *Tape the stencil over one of the squares on the grid. Stencil all the yellow circles and surrounds, then stencil the red circles and surrounds.*

four *Touch up any smudges with the artist's brush. When the paint is completely dry, rub out any visible pencil lines.*

five *Apply a coat of varnish. Attach the wall-board to the wall by inserting screw eyelets and stringing picture-hanging wire between them. Hammer in a strong picture hook and hang the board as you would a painting. Alternatively, drill holes in the wall and insert plastic anchors, screw the board to the wall and fill and make good the screw holes.*

LIVING ROOM SECRETS

JUST BECAUSE YOU INVEST heavily in some great curtain fabric, you should not feel committed to spending at least as much again on having it made up. This is a totally no-sew curtain and valance idea that could easily pass for the work of a professional. To figure out how much material you need, just measure the drop and allow three times that length. The seams are all iron-on and the rest is done with a staple gun and string. It's hard to imagine that such an elegant draped valance could be put together without sewing a stitch. Follow the steps to discover the hidden secrets that lie behind this living room window.

YOU WILL NEED

striped fabric

tape measure

scissors

iron-on hem tape or double-sided carpet tape (optional)

iron

2 narrow strips wood, window width, plus 12 inches each side

level

drill

plastic anchors and screws

screwdriver

staple gun

string

one *Divide the fabric into three equal lengths, two for the curtains and one for the valance. Turn over the hems on both ends of the valance and one end of each of the curtains. Attach the hems with iron-on hem tape, or carpet tape if the fabric is very heavy. Attach the thin side of one of the strips of wood to the wall so that the ends overlap the window equally—use a level to check the position. Screw the other strip of wood onto it at a right angle.* ➤

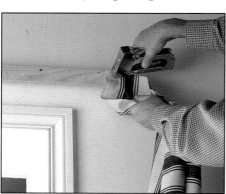

two *Starting at one end, staple the edge of one curtain to the front of the strip of wood. Staple the other corner of the curtain to the middle of the wood. Most of the curtain will now hang loose in the middle.*

three *For the pleats, hold the curtain away from the window and find the middle. Staple this to the middle of the wood. Find the middle of the two loose sections and staple them to the middle of the strip of wood. Keep subdividing the strip of wood and the fabric until you have reached the pleat width you want. Repeat for the other curtain.*

four *Fold the valance fabric in half lengthwise and line up with the center of the window. Starting at the center, staple along one edge to the top of the strip of wood, close to the wall. Lift the side drops and gather up the fabric at the corners. Put a row of staples under the gather so that the stripes line up with the curtain stripes below.*

five *Bunch up the fabric at each corner and tie it with string. Be aware of the way the fabric folds at this stage —you may need to practice folding and tying a few times until you achieve the desired effect. Staple the string to the strip of wood. It won't show, so use as many staples as you need to make it secure.*

six *Tie another piece of string around the drop of the valance, about 12 inches down. Tie it tightly, leaving enough string to let you tie another knot to raise this section to the top corner.*

seven *Pull the fabric up to the corner and tie the string ends tightly around the first knot. Push the knots inside the remaining fabric to puff the front out. If necessary, add staples to hold this in place along the top of the strip of wood. Finally, arrange the pleats and folds.*

No-Frills Navy

BLOCK OUT THE LIGHT with these crisp, stylish navy blue curtains. Cotton canvas is as heavy as denim, but to add firmness and thickness to the tops, you can use double-sided carpet tape to bond them together. This also means that you get a good fit with the large brass eyelets that are made for tent canvas and sails. You will need to buy fabric about one-and-a-half times the width of your window plus an allowance of 2 inches at the top and bottom to get perfect pleats. It is always a good idea to err on the generous side with curtains, so stretch the budget rather than the fabric on this project.

YOU WILL NEED

double-sided carpet tape
craft knife
navy cotton canvas
backing cardboard
ruler
pencil
hole punch
hammer
brass eyelets
rigging wire, window width
2 wire rope grips
2 thimbles
pliers
drill
2 plastic anchors and large hooks

one *Stick a length of double-sided carpet tape along the top of the fabric, just in from the edge. Peel off the top paper. Fold the top hem over the tape, smoothing as you go to ensure a crisp, wrinkle-free finish.*

two *Place the curtain on a sheet of backing cardboard. Using a ruler and a pencil, mark the positions for the holes at 8-inch intervals. Put the back part of the hole punch in position behind the fabric to make the first hole.*

three *Position the top part of the hole punch and bang it firmly with a hammer. Place the back part of the eyelet in the back part of the hole punch. Place the middle of the eyelet through the punched hole.*

four *Place the top half of the eyelet on top of the bottom half. Position the tool provided with the eyelets and bang it firmly with a hammer. Continue positioning the eyelets at the marked intervals along the top of the curtains.*

five *Thread the rigging wire through the wire grip to form a loop. Place the thimble inside the loop and pull the wire taut. Using a hammer on a hard surface, bang the wire grip closed. You may also need to squeeze it with pliers.*

six *Drill holes and attach one of the hooks in the window recess. Loop the rigging wire over it. Thread the curtains onto the rigging wire through the eyelets.*

seven *Thread the other end through the wire grip as before, then attach to a hook. Screw the hook into a pre-drilled and plugged hole. This will ensure even pleats.*

PRIMARY PLASTIC

THIN SHEETS OF OPAQUE, colored plastic, which are available from art supply stores, make excellent lampshade materials. They are available in a range of colors, and the edges can be cut decoratively, with no need for seaming, and fastened in place with nuts and bolts. As plastic is a fairly rigid material, it does not require a supporting frame, although you can use one for a template if desired.

YOU WILL NEED

brown paper

spray adhesive

sheets of red and yellow plastic

craft knife

cutting mat

pen

ruler

broad cloth tape

masking tape

wood block

drill, with twist bit

nuts and bolts

shade carrier (optional)

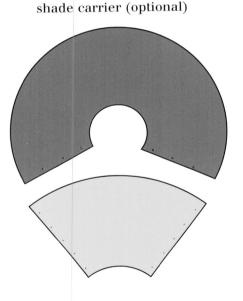

RED SHADE

one *Enlarge the template. Transfer it onto brown paper. Spray the back with adhesive and stick it onto the red sheet. Cut out the shade with a craft knife. Make a cardboard template for the sawtooth pattern. Place it on the edge of the brown-paper pattern, on the plastic sheet, and draw around it.*

two *Cut out the border. Cut toward the outside edge every time. Remove the paper and attach the long edges of the shade with cloth tape. Place a strip of masking tape along this seam. Place the wood block behind the seam, then drill three holes through the plastic. Remove the tape and screw in the nuts and bolts.*

YELLOW SHADE

one *Enlarge the template and transfer it to brown paper. Spray the back with adhesive and stick it onto a sheet of yellow plastic. Place on the cutting mat and cut out the shade using a craft knife.*

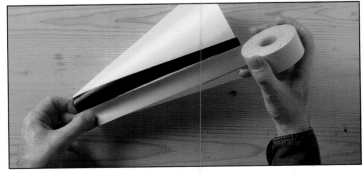

two *Overlap the two long edges of the shade and secure with a strip of cloth tape. Then place a strip of masking tape along this seam.*

three *Using a ruler, mark five equal divisions along the seam. Place a wood block behind the seam and carefully drill a hole through the plastic at each mark. Start peeling off the tape at the top of the shade and screw in a nut and bolt each time a drilled hole is exposed.*

DRAPED DIRECTOR'S CHAIR

COMPLETELY DRAPED IN A slip cover, a folding director's chair loses its functional character and takes on the role of an armchair. Avoid complicated fitting by cutting a simple tunic-style slip cover, based on squares and rectangles that are just tied together. You can then put the cover straight onto the chair without ironing, since it can be removed and stored flat when the chair is folded away.

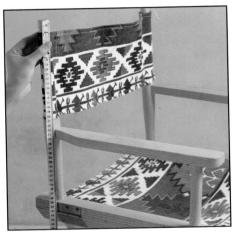

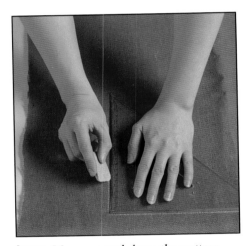

one *Measure: (a) from floor to top edge of back; (b) from top edge of back to back of seat; (c) length of seat; (d) width of seat; (e) from center of wooden armrest to inside base of seat; (f) from center of armrest to floor; (g) from front edge of seat to floor.*

two *Measure and draw the pattern pieces directly onto the fabric, with a seam allowance all around each piece. Cut out, then pin, baste and sew the pieces together following the diagram at the back of the book.*

three *Mark and cut strips of fabric to make ties of a finished size of about 1 inch wide and 16 inches long. Put right sides together and sew the long edges together. Then turn them out and slip-stitch the ends.*

four *Assemble the tunic as a cross (see diagram). Slip the finished cover over the chair and knot the ties firmly.*

ℒACED DINING CHAIR

Tʀᴀɴsғᴏʀᴍ ᴀ ᴅᴜʟʟ ᴄʜᴀɪʀ into a modern piece with added comfort and dramatic color. These covers can be permanent or changed at whim. Any bright canvas fabric is suitable; economic cotton canvas has been used here. The fabric must have a little body or you will need to add a backing fabric. Ticking, canvas or linen are all suitable.

Self-covering buttons with cord loops or, for the more skilled, buttonholes are good alternatives to lacing eyelets. Loops and toggles or frogging give a military look, especially with a bright scarlet fabric.

YOU WILL NEED

dining chair

measuring tape

foam or rubberized horse hair (to fit the back of the chair)

scissors

tape for ties

thin batting (to fit the back of the chair)

upholstery tacks

tissue or pattern-cutting paper

felt-tipped pen

3 yards of 50-inch-wide cotton canvas

dressmaker's pins

sewing machine

matching thread

iron

safety pins

fabric marker

hole-punching tool

hammer

8 eyelets

eyelet pliers

3 yards cotton tape

one *Measure the chair back for the size of the foam backing or rubberized horse hair. Cut the backing to size and attach it to the chair back with ties at the top and bottom.*

two *Cover the foam or horse hair loosely with thin batting and secure the batting with tacks.*

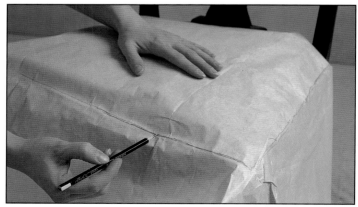

three *Lay the pattern-cutting paper on the seat and draw around it, adding a 1½-inch seam allowance. Make a pattern for the front of the seat back.*

four *Decide how deep the skirt will be, then figure out the dimensions for the back. The back panel incorporates a box pleat to allow easy removal (see diagram). Draw a pattern.*

five *For the skirt, measure the two sides and front of the seat, then add 12 inches for each of the four box pleats. Add 1½ inches to the depth as a seam allowance. Make a pattern.*

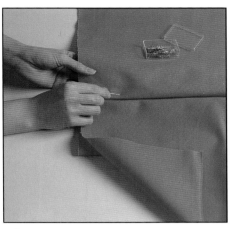

six *Lay the patterns on your material and cut out each piece. Take the back panel and pin, then stitch the central box pleat down to 1½ inches from the top of the seat and press it.*

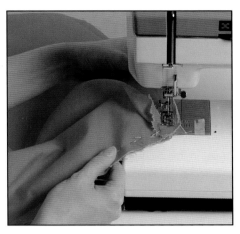

seven *Stitch the front panel to the top of the seat panel with the right sides together. Trim and press open all the seams as you go.*

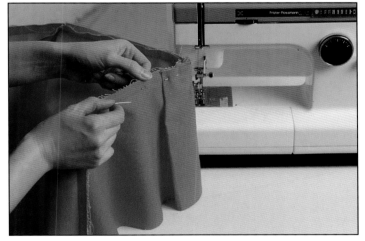

eight *Stitch the front panel to the back at the top and sides. Hem the bottom edge of the skirt. Fold and pin the box pleats so they fall in the corners of the seat. Machine-stitch the seat and skirt in place along the top edges.*

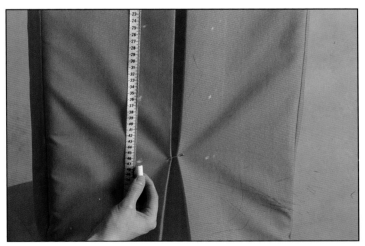

nine *Put the cover on the seat, close the back pleat with safety pins and mark where the eyelets are to be with a fabric marker.*

ten *Remove the cover. Using a hole-punching tool, make holes for the eyelets.*

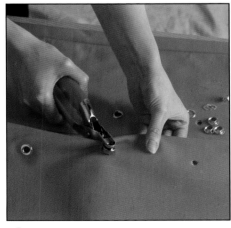

eleven *Following the manufacturer's instructions, attach the eyelets.*

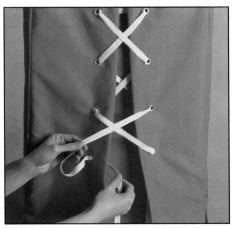

twelve *Put the cover on the chair and lace up the back with cotton tape.*

CONTINUED OVER ➤

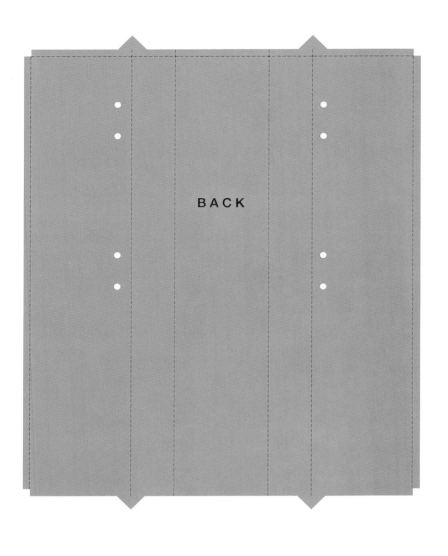

BACK

FRONT

SEAT

EDGING

DINING CHAIR

THE EFFECT IS STYLISH and practical and yet needs no sewing skills. None of the usual difficulties caused by the need for washing of fitted covers apply, so you can capitalize on the sheer drama that is created by stark white. A generous quantity of fabric is the only essential; this project uses a king-size pure cotton sheet, which is already hemmed, but you can use any wide, preferably washable, fabric that is soft enough to knot and tie.

YOU WILL NEED

chair

fabric

sewing machine (optional)

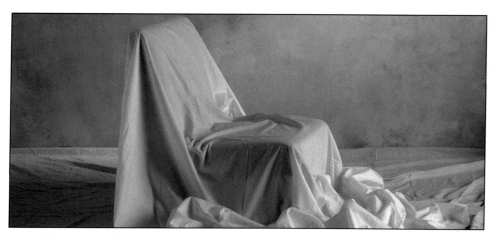

one *You need at least twice, and preferably three times, as much fabric as the width of your chair. Hem the fabric, if necessary. Throw the fabric over the chair and center it.*

two *Tuck the fabric down the back behind the seat of the chair. If the chair has arms, do this all around the seat, so that the cover doesn't pull when you sit on the chair.*

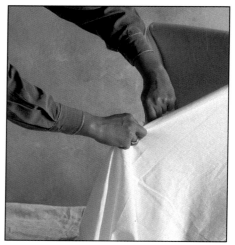

three *Sweep the fabric around to the back of the chair.*

four *Tie a knot, making sure that the fabric is an even length on both sides and that you have attractive folds and drapes at the sides. Try to tie the knot confidently the first time; otherwise the fabric will get wrinkled. Remember that the fabric should cascade down from the knot.*

PARQUET

GOOD PARQUET IS A very manageable kind of flooring. There are numerous patterns to be made from combining these wooden blocks. One good technique is to figure out the pattern starting from the center and make it as big a perfect square as you can, then lay a simple border to accommodate all the tricky outside edges. Parquet is often in oak but you could dye it with stain or varnish for a richer effect.

YOU WILL NEED
string
pencil
ridged adhesive spreader
floor adhesive
parquet blocks
strip of wood
matte varnish
paintbrush
fine-grade sandpaper

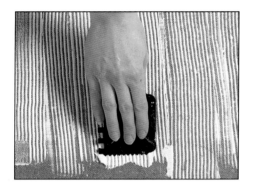

one *Make sure your floor surface is clean, dry and level. Find your starting point by stretching string from corner to corner as for tiles and draw guidelines on the floor. Using a ridged spreader, coat a small area of floor with adhesive.*

two *Apply parquet blocks to the adhesive. Use a strip of wood laid across the blocks to check that they all lie flush. Repeat until the floor is covered. Seal the floor with two or three coats of varnish, sanding between coats.*

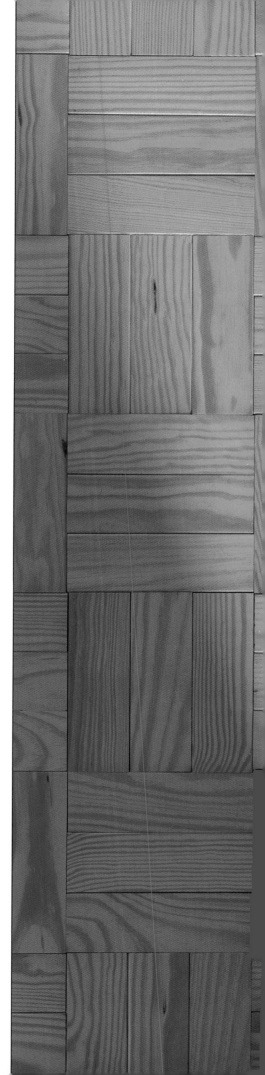

GROOVY FLOOR

TONGUE-AND-GROOVE BOARDS look wonderful with a gleaming shine. Gloss paint or floor paint is durable and easily renewed if it's ever damaged. Use this floor in a room with a large window and enjoy the dramatic effect of the sun streaming across it. Gloss paint shows up detail, so it was a natural choice for these brand new tongue-and-groove boards but, if you like the effect of the dramatic color but have an old floor, a matte finish would be more forgiving. To lay a new floor of this type, a perfectly smooth and level subfloor is vital.

YOU WILL NEED

tongue-and-groove boards
hammer
drill, with pilot drill bit
flooring pins
pin hammer
nail punch
power sander and sandpaper
undercoat and paintbrushes
high-gloss floor paint

one *Slot the tongue-and-groove boards together and, using a scrap of wood to protect the exposed tongue, tap the next board into place until it fits tightly. If the boards are warped, pin one end first and work along the board; in this way you will be able to straighten out the warp.*

two *To prevent the tongues from splitting, pre-drill pilot holes. Tap pins in gently, using a pin hammer, at a slight angle back toward the boards.*

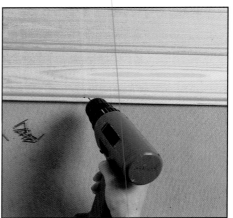

three *Punch the pins in with a nail punch so the next board can butt up.*

four *When the floor is laid, and before finishing it, sand it, first with a coarse-grade sandpaper and then with medium-grade and finally with fine-grade. Always sand in line with the wood grain. With long, even strokes, in line with the boards, undercoat the floor. Leave to dry. Lightly sand again and paint with gloss paint.*

JEWEL-BRIGHT ARMCHAIR

MANY ELEGANTLY SHAPED armchairs are disguised beneath several layers of ugly orange or dark brown varnish and dowdy upholstery fabrics. Once the covers have been removed and the old varnish has been sanded away, however, these chairs can be transformed instantly into desirable objects. Stretchy fabrics make it easier to achieve a neat, professional finish, but any upholstery fabric is suitable.

YOU WILL NEED
armchair
medium-grade sandpaper
clear wax or silicone polish
rubber fabric
scissors
staple gun
rubber adhesive
paintbrush
hammer
upholstery tacks
thick artist's cardboard

one *Remove all the old covers. Sand the varnish from the frame. Seal with clear wax or silicone polish. Using the existing cover pieces as patterns, cut the fabric to the size of the back rest, with a generous allowance to turn to the back surface. Stretch it over the back rest until it is hand-tight and staple it in place. Secure, in order, the top, bottom and sides, with one or two staples in the center, before applying lines of staples to keep the fabric taut.*

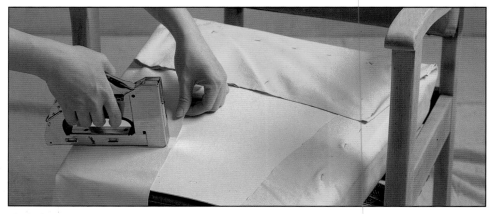

two *Cut a piece of fabric to fit the back surface of the backrest and use rubber adhesive to stick the fabric to the chair so that it covers the staples and the turned-over edges of the first layer. Hammer a tack into each corner.*

three *For the cushion, trace its shape onto the cardboard. Cut out and staple to the cushion. Wrap the fabric around the cushion, tucking in the corners neatly, and staple to the cardboard. Attach a layer of fabric to the underside of the cushion (following step 2), using rubber adhesive.*

BOLD BLOCKS OF COLOR

FOR THE BOLDEST LOOK of all, paint vibrant blocks of color all over the walls to create an effect like a painting by the Dutch Cubist Piet Mondrian. Using a basic square grid, work across and up and down to create strong patterns and changes of color. Although this example has been created in very brightly colored paints, you could choose a more subdued or even subtle look, using complementary tones or much paler colors. Use this effect on all the walls in a room, if you're feeling brave, or confine it to one area, such as above a chair-rail in a hall, for a less intense effect.

YOU WILL NEED

level

straightedge

pencil

scrap paper

latex paint in several colors

small and medium
paintbrushes

masking tape

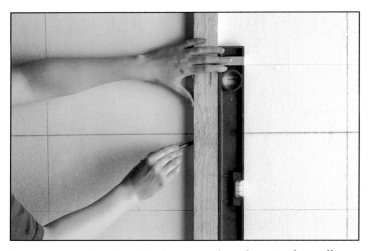

one *Draw a basic grid of squares directly onto the wall, using the level, straightedge and pencil.*

two *Decide on your colors. Putting small samples together on a sheet of paper may help you to decide which ones work together best.*

three *Mask off the areas for the first color. The blocks can be squares or oblongs, and they can turn corners. Use as many or as few squares of the grid as you like.*

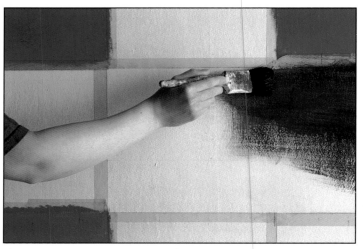

four *Paint the blocks. Remove the tape immediately and let dry. Repeat the process for each of the subsequent colors in your scheme.*

FLOATING FLOOR

WOOD-STRIP FLOORING IS a good way of creating instant elegance. It comes in a huge variety of finishes and lengths, so you can combine different woods without difficulty. Once you have mastered the principles of how to lay it, you can work out many different combinations and patterns. The main photograph shows walnut interspersed with wide, light-colored maple boards. Alternatively, choose just one wood and lay it in different patterns. Laminated types of wood strip are generally pre-finished but others need to be sealed once they have been laid.

YOU WILL NEED

cushioned underlay
(if necessary)

tape

metal joint clips

hammer

wood-strip flooring

spacers

wood glue

saw

tacks and quadrant beading
(optional)

pencil

drill, with wood bit

one *If you are using underlay, unroll it and tape one end to keep it in place. Prepare all the boards of wood-strip by hammering the special metal joint clips into the groove on the underside of the board, along the tongued edge.*

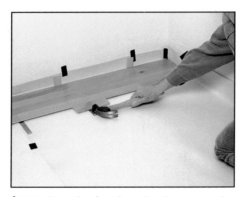

two *Lay the first length, clips toward you, against the walls, using spacers. Glue the ends of butt-jointed lengths. Position the second row of boards, tapping them together with a hammer and a scrap of wood, so that the clips engage in the groove of the second row.*

three *Cut the last board to width, allowing for spacers, and apply glue along its grooved edge. Insert, packing against the wall before levering the strip into place. Hammer it down level, using a scrap of wood for protection.*

four *Replace the skirtings or tack lengths of quadrant beading to hide the expansion gap; make sure the skirting fits tightly against the floor.*

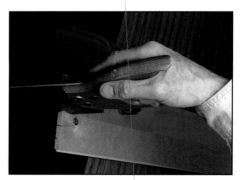

five *To fit a board around a pipe, mark its position and drill a suitably sized hole. Then cut out a tapered wedge, which can be glued back after placing the board.*

SPRIGGED CURTAINS

NATURAL CALICO HAS A lovely creamy color, especially when the sun shines through it. However, it is usually used as a lining fabric, and this association can make it look unfinished. This stamped floral sprig lifts the humble calico into another dimension, giving it a sophisticated finish. Calico is prone to shrinkage, so wash the fabric before you stamp it and make the curtains. The design for the calico stamp is in the template section at the back of the book.

YOU WILL NEED
calico fabric
linoleum block stamp
scrap paper
fabric ink: green and dark blue
scalpel
ruler
cardboard
pencil

one *Lay the fabric out on a flat surface, such as a wallpaper-pasting table. Make several prints of the linoleum block stamp on scrap paper, cut them out with a scalpel and use them to plan the position of the motifs on the fabric.*

two *Decide on the distance between the sprigs, and cut out a square of cardboard with the same dimensions to act as a measuring guide. Use it diagonally, making a pencil mark at each corner over the surface of the fabric.*

three *Apply green ink directly to the edges of the linoleum block stamp. Fill in the middle of the stamp with dark blue ink. Make an initial print on a scrap of fabric to determine the density of the stamped image.*

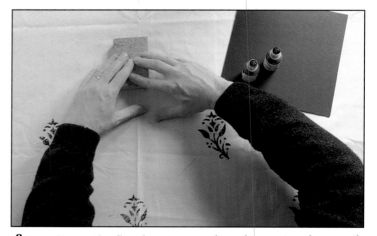

four *Stamp the floral sprig onto the calico, using the pencil marks to position the base of the stamp. You need to apply gentle pressure to the back of the stamp and allow a couple of seconds for the ink to transfer. Don't rush; the result will be all the better for the extra time taken.*

DISTRESSED FLOORBOARDS

OLD WOODEN FLOORS ARE often appealing because of their subtle variations of color. Wood stains can help to imitate that look in only a few hours. The look of driftwood or weathered teak or other hardwood decking, like that of beach houses, is the aim. Achieve the outdoor look using three different wood stains and a wash of white latex, diluted almost to water. This technique would give a bleached effect to any wood stain.

YOU WILL NEED

nail punch

hammer

power sander and fine-grade sandpaper

wire brush

3 different wood stains of the same make

lint-free cloth or paintbrushes

rubber gloves

latex paint: white or cream

dry cloth

matte polyurethane floor varnish

one *It is important that floors have no sharp or protruding nails, so knock in any you find with a nail punch before you begin. Remove old paint spills using a sander. Remember to change the sandpaper frequently, or you will damage the rubber seal of the sander.*

two *Brush the boards with a wire brush, along the direction of the grain, with the occasional contrasting stroke to give a distressed effect. Experiment with the stains, combining colors—a little should go a long way. Use scrap wood to test the effect before you commit yourself by staining the floor.*

three *With either a lint-free cloth or a paintbrush, apply the stain. This will stain anything porous, so wear rubber gloves and old clothes.*

four *Start by applying quite a generous quantity of stain, but rub most of the surplus off. Don't stop until you've finished the floor or there will be a definite line; keep the seams between areas random and avoid overlapping parallel bands of stain.*

five *It is better to do one thin coat all over and then go back to apply additional coats. To give an uneven, weathered look you can work the stain into the knots or grooves with a brush.*

six *While the stain is still wet, brush on a wash of the diluted white or cream paint, about one part latex to four parts water.*

seven *Using a dry cloth, rub off the surplus or apply more until you have the effect you want.*

eight *Apply at least two coats of varnish, sanding very lightly between coats.*

CONTEMPORARY SHELF

ALTHOUGH NURSERY METHODS have been employed to decorate this shelf, the result is an incredibly sophisticated room feature. The shelf pattern has been cut into one half of a potato, with all the colors painted on at the same time, to allow one-step printing. A row of potato stamps like this has a three-dimensional quality, which is enhanced by the choice and positioning of the colors. This is an easy project to carry out, which has an effect far beyond its simple origins. Experiment with other color schemes if you prefer.

YOU WILL NEED
ruler
potato
felt-tipped pen
scalpel
knife
gouache, poster or acrylic paint: red, light blue, dark blue, green and yellow
paintbrushes

one *Measure the width of the shelf edge and cut the potato to fit. Draw the simple pattern shapes onto the potato. Cut down with a scalpel to outline the shape, then cut across with a knife to remove the background.*

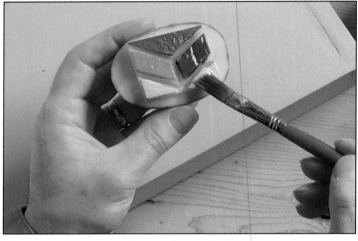

two *Mix the paint, then apply each color to a separate part of the design with a paintbrush.*

three *Begin printing the shelf edge, making the first print on the short side section that will be nearest the wall.*

four *Continue to apply the paint as before and stamp the pattern to cover all the shelf edges.*

STUDIES AND HALLWAYS

STUDIES AND HALLWAYS ARE OFTEN the most neglected areas of the house, repositories for everything that cannot find a home elsewhere. No wonder that sometimes these spaces look messy. They needn't — and you don't have to throw out everything and start again. The clever way to transform these areas is to use what you already have.

The hallway, in particular, is an important space. It provides that lasting first impression in any house and should give a hint of what lies beyond. There is little sense, after all, in having wonderfully light and bright rooms linked by a gloomy hallway crammed full of mismatched furniture.

Studies and dens can be hard to get right simply because they often need to double as TV rooms, spare bedrooms or playrooms. Decorated to reflect your personality, they can be havens for work and creative passions, while still retaining their multiple functions.

Mismatched though everything may be, you can still make everything look coordinated. Light fittings and lampshades, even the lounge chair that has seen better days: All can be given a fresh new look that makes them fit in perfectly.

The style of lighting reflects the whole mood of the house. With a little imagination there are many designs that can be used to make decorative lampshades at minimal cost.

Imagine what you can put on the walls of these rooms! A big wall map given a coat of tinted varnish makes any study look like a million dollars. Wallpaper can be fun too, especially when you customize it or even make your own. The Escher-inspired wall covering of gray and black geometric patterns looks sensational and is really very easy to do.

You can even use a photocopier, creating striking wall treatments at the push of a button. Take a favorite subject, make lots of photocopies, cut them out and glue them onto the wall. It's hard to imagine that anything so simple could look so good and produce such successful decorative results.

WILD WEST CHAIR

IF YOU HAVE AN old armchair of these robust proportions, it will lend itself to this fun treatment reminiscent of the pioneer days of the Wild West. Update it with animal-skin prints and leather fringing for a new and imaginative look, as well as a cozy and comfortable feel. You could also use leatherette for the cushion covers or blankets, which would still be in keeping with this chunky, masculine look.

YOU WILL NEED
armchair
fake-fur or animal-skin fabric
upholstery needle
strong thread
tape measure
leather or suede
self-healing cutting mat
ruler
craft knife
leather glue
double-sided tape
pencil
softwood block
studs
hammer
rubber or softwood scrap

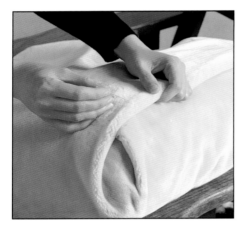

one *Remove the seat cushions of the armchair and wrap in fake-fur or animal-skin fabric, leaving sufficient fabric to make a continuous flap the length of the cushion. Stitch securely. Decide on the length of fringing needed to decorate the inside and outside edges of the arms of the chair.*

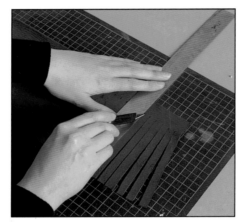

two *Decide how deep you want the fringe on the leather or suede to be. Measure and cut the fringe with a craft knife on a cutting mat, leaving sufficient uncut material to make a hem. Apply glue to the edge of the leather or suede and fold over the hem. Press it down firmly.*

three *Apply double-sided tape to the chair arms and stick on the fringing, matching it on both arms.*

four *Mark the positions of the studs with a pencil, using a block of wood to gauge the distance between each. Position the studs with your thumb, press and then tap with a hammer, protecting the stud with a scrap of rubber or a piece of softwood.*

Skewbald Shade

A SKEWBALD PATTERN—brown patches on a white pony—is perhaps the boldest of animal-skin prints and always makes a strong style statement. It is very adaptable and can be used in a contemporary, minimalist room, a child's bedroom, a study or as a classic Tex-Mex decorating style. Brown packing paper is strong and makes satisfactory stencils; the shapes of the patches need to be irregular to imitate the unique character of a skewbald pattern.

YOU WILL NEED

felt-tipped pen
brown packing paper
scalpel
cutting mat
spray adhesive
plain fabric lampshade
brown acrylic paint
paintbrush
glue gun with all-purpose
glue sticks
brown fringing

one *Draw irregular cloud-like shapes on brown packing paper. You need several small ones and a bigger one. Keep the shapes curved, with no sharp angles. Use a scalpel to cut out the stencils.*

two *Spray the backs of the stencils very lightly with adhesive and arrange them on the shade. Position the large shape to overlap the rim. Stencil the brown shapes onto the shade, working inward from the edges and making sure the paint gets into the weave of the fabric.*

three *Stencil the larger shape right up against any edging strip, or over the rim of the shade. The pattern will appear more natural if you do it this way. Use the glue gun to stick the fringing around the bottom rim.*

DUSTPAN TIDY

IF YOU HAVE TO excavate piles of paper, notebooks, lists and old letters every time you need a pen, then it is time to get the dustpans out. This project gives a new meaning to tidying up. Two metal dustpans can be spray-painted to match or in any color combination and attached with bolts. Use the dustpans for stationery, a small paper tray or, perhaps most suitably, for filing bills.

YOU WILL NEED

2 metal dustpans

4 metal washers

enamel car spray paint: lime green and metallic blue

newspaper

G-clamp

2 pieces corrugated cardboard

pencil

drill, with metal bit

2 nuts and bolts

pliers

screwdriver

one *Spray one dustpan and two washers lime green and the others metallic blue. Protect your work surface with newspaper and build up the color gradually with light puffs of paint. Let dry.*

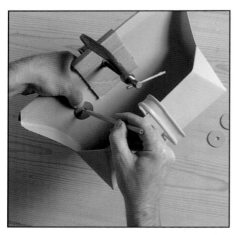

two *Clamp the dustpans together, protecting the paintwork with cardboard. Hold the washers at the point where the dustpans meet and mark two equal positions with a pencil.*

three *Drill through the marks on both dustpans. Place a washer on either side of a hole, hold the nut with pliers and tighten the bolt with a screwdriver. Repeat for the other hole.*

EASTERN PROMISE

DIRECTOR'S CHAIRS ARE INEXPENSIVE, but because the backrest and the seat are made of cloth they are very comfortable. Plain canvas seats are the standard form, but by customizing you can create a fun and rather chic effect. Kilim fabric is very long-lasting and has beautiful muted colors derived from traditional carpet designs, but any fabric that is strong and without too much "give" can be used; tapestry, burlap or carpet are all suitable. For even more character, stain the frame of the chair to match the muted tones of the kilim.

YOU WILL NEED

director's chair

wood stain and paintbrush (optional)

kilim carpet or fabric

dressmaker's pins

scissors

large darning or upholstery needle

strong darning yarn

package of chrome studs (at least 6)

hammer

one *Remove the old seat and back of the chair. Stain the wood of the chair, if desired. Choose the most decorative part of the kilim carpet or fabric and pin the old fabric to it as a pattern. Carefully cut out new seat and back pieces.*

two *Thread the needle with the yarn and neatly blanket-stitch the edges to bind them.*

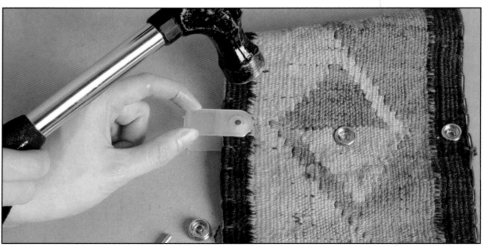

three *Fold over the edges of the back and fasten with chrome poppers, then slip over the uprights. Slot the seat back into position and secure firmly.*

MINIMALIST CHAIR

SLEEK BEECH AND CHROME chairs abound in interiors magazines—with price tags to match. This makes renovating old chairs a very rewarding proposition. Most second-hand office-supply stores have lots of worn-out office chairs, often with torn upholstery or in hideous colors. Don't be drawn to a more modern chair that appears in a better state but has plastic-coated legs; metal legs look better when renovated.

YOU WILL NEED

old typist's chair
scissors
screwdriver or awl
pliers
industrial rubber gloves
chemical paint stripper
1–2-inch brush
steel wool
soap
medium-grade sandpaper
all-in-one stain and varnish
hammer
"domes of silence"
metal or chrome polish
soft, dry cloth

one *Start by cutting off excess fabric and foam. You need strong scissors with large plastic handles to avoid hurting your hands. Remove the fabric and upholstery staples from the back and underside of the chair. Use the screwdriver or awl for the hard-to-reach parts and the pliers to pull out the old staples.*

two *Remove the wheels and any other loose parts to prevent them from being damaged by the paint stripper. Wearing the industrial rubber gloves, brush the paint stripper onto the metal chair frame. Set aside for 5 minutes (or as long as the manufacturer recommends) and then wash off with steel wool and soapy water. Repeat until all the paint has been removed.*

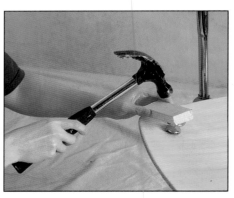

three *Having removed the seat and back, make sure the surfaces are free of nails and staples. Sand the surfaces and edges of the seat and back until they are smooth and clean. Seal the wood with all-in-one stain and varnish, and let dry.*

four *Reattach the seat, back and wheels. Use "domes of silence" to cover any sharp bolts that might rip your clothes. Finally, polish the metal using a soft, dry cloth.*

ANTIQUE MAP

MAPS ARE BOTH FASCINATING to study and extremely decorative, and this makes them wonderful for covering walls. Choose an up-to-date map for a child's room to maximize the learning possibilities. Elsewhere in the house, "antique" or old Ordnance Survey local area maps will look terrific and create an eye-catching focal point. You can easily distress a new map to give it an aged appearance. You could even paper a whole wall in maps—perhaps of geographically adjoining areas.

YOU WILL NEED

tape measure
pencil
straightedge
level or plumb line
map
wallpaper paste
pasting brush
fine-grade sandpaper
tinted varnish
paintbrush

one *Measure and mark guidelines for positioning the map on the wall, using a straightedge and a level or plumb line. Paste the map to the wall as if it were wallpaper.*

two *Distress the map here and there by lightly rubbing it with sandpaper. Finish the aging process by applying a coat of tinted varnish.*

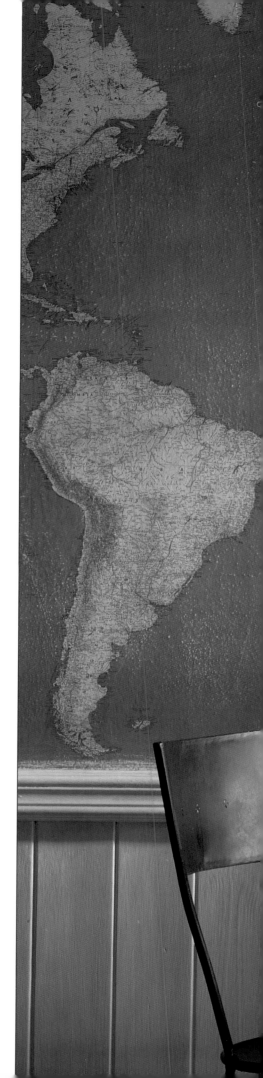

MATH MONTAGE

THIS IS A FUN idea for adding interest to a plain wall. The numbers and mathematical symbols have been enlarged on a photocopier. It doesn't matter if the black becomes streaked with white as the number is enlarged: This enhances the handcrafted look. It is most effective if you confine the montage to a set area, such as behind a desk, for maximum effect; just let the design fall away at the edges. You could also try musical notation behind a piano or shorthand characters in an office.

YOU WILL NEED
craft knife
self-healing cutting mat
masking tape
wallpaper paste
pasting brush
artist's paintbrush
clear varnish
varnish brush

one *Photocopy the numbers and symbols from the templates at the back of the book and enlarge them to various sizes. Cut them out carefully with the craft knife on the cutting mat.*

two *Try out the design first by attaching the shapes to the wall using small pieces of masking tape; move them around until you are satisfied. Alternatively, simply start and figure out the design as you go. Paste the shapes onto the wall using wallpaper paste. Use the artist's brush to paste small and delicate shapes. Give the whole design a coat of varnish, to protect it.*

1

3+5=8

+

1

3

(6)

5

90

$$L = \frac{2\pi Ma}{\lambda T}$$

4−3=1

5

÷

8

9

7

2

4

6

2

8

ESCHER-STYLE WALL

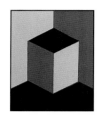

INTRICATE "THREE-DIMENSIONAL" designs, inspired by the *trompe-l'œil* drawings of the artist M.C. Escher, look stunning on a wall on which you want to make a real impact. The instructions for how to construct the design sound complicated but, in fact, once you have begun cutting out and assembling it, it soon becomes obvious how the shapes fit together. The beauty of Escher's designs is that all the components relate logically to one another in proportion and shape so that, once you have begun construction, the design practically assembles itself.

YOU WILL NEED
scrap paper

pencil

metal ruler

paper: light gray, dark gray and black

craft knife

self-healing cutting mat

straightedge

level or plumb line

wallpaper paste

pasting brush

clear varnish

varnish brush

one *Plan and draw the whole pattern to scale on paper or refer to the diagram at the back of the book. Decide on the colors of paper you want to use; choose three tones of the same color to achieve a three-dimensional effect. Measure the paper. Divide a sheet of the light gray paper into thirds.*

two *Measure in from the edge to the depth of the large gray triangle shapes that form the border and mark the points of the triangles.*

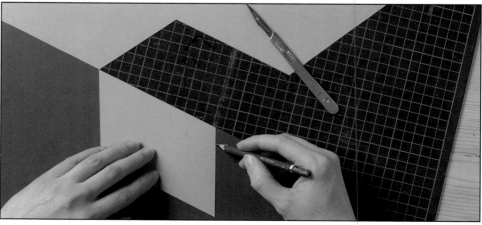

three *Draw the diagonals to make the triangle shapes. Cut out the large light and dark gray triangles and then the diamond shapes, using the craft knife on a cutting mat. You will find that, once you have cut one shape, you will be able to use it as a template for others, because of the way the shapes relate to one another.*

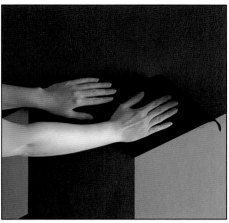

four *Draw the smaller light and dark gray diamonds that make two "sides" of the small "boxes." Cut out the smaller diamonds. Cut out the large and small black shapes.*

five *Using a level or plumb line and straightedge, draw vertical lines on the wall the same width as the large gray shapes.*

six *Paste all the shapes into place using wallpaper paste and pasting brush. Smooth out any wrinkles with the palms of your hands. Give the design two coats of protective varnish.*

ESCHER'S DECKCHAIR

DECKCHAIRS ARE CHEAP and widely available in several styles. The slings are usually canvas, available at furniture stores in a variety of brightly colored plain and striped materials. Deckchair canvas comes in the correct width and with ready-sealed edges. To give an old deckchair a new lease on life, use a pattern of stencils, or turn checks into a "three-dimensional" puzzle. This design is based on M.C. Escher's work and is made from a combination of positive and negative motifs.

YOU WILL NEED
deckchair
deckchair canvas
scissors
spray adhesive
high-density foam
craft knife
self-healing cutting mat
ruler or triangle
colored tape
pencil
fabric paint: black and white
paintbrush
needle
matching thread

one *Remove the old sling, making a note of how it was fastened so that you can fasten it in the same way later. Using the old cover as a pattern, cut out the new fabric, allowing for hems along the top and bottom edges.*

two *To make the two stamps for printing, photocopy the motifs from the back of the book to the desired size. Stick to the foam with spray adhesive. Cut around the design with the craft knife.*

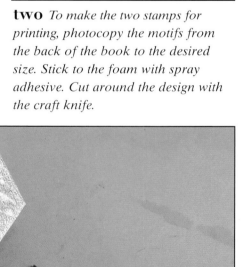

three *Using the knife, chip away the zigzag shape between the dotted lines to leave two elements of the design distinct. Remove all the foam that is not part of the "negative" design. It is helpful to mark the backs of the stamps with colored tape to indicate which color paint is used with which stamp. Repeat steps 2 and 3 to make the "positive" stamp.*

four *Using a ruler and pencil, draw parallel lines lengthwise on the canvas, the distance between them equalling the full width of the design when the two stamps are put together (see step 7).*

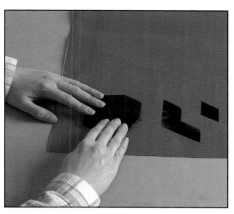

five *Apply the black paint to the raised portion of one of the stamps.*

six *Applying light, even pressure, stamp the black design regularly within the grid lines.*

seven *Repeat with the white design. When dry, hem the top and bottom edges of the canvas, then fasten to the chair frame.*

TRELLIS HANGING RACK

A GARDEN TRELLIS MAKES AN effective hanging rack. Extend the trellis to make regular diamond shapes and then frame it with wood to give a finished look. You could confine this idea to a small area or attach a few pieces of trellis together to run the whole length of a wall. Put hooks on as many crossovers as you want, and collect decorative items, as well as more mundane utilitarian objects, to add to the display. Move things from time to time, so the display always offers something new to catch the eye.

YOU WILL NEED

tape measure

pencil

length of garden trellis

hacksaw

1 x 1 inch strips wood

miter block and saw or miter saw

dowel

wood screws

screwdriver

drill, with wood, metal and masonry bits

burnt-orange latex paint

paintbrush

plastic anchors

wood filler

one *Measure the area you want to cover and mark out the area on the trellis. Cut the trellis to size with a hacksaw. Measure and cut the lengths of wood to make the frame. Miter the corners using a miter block or miter saw. Screw the frame together.*

two *Mark the dowel into lengths and cut a notch in each length, for hanging hooks. Cut the dowel into lengths, using the miter block or miter saw.*

three *If the trellis is riveted at the crossovers, drill the rivets out. Position the dowel pegs on the trellis over the crossovers. Screw the pegs to the trellis. Paint the trellis and the frame with latex paint in your chosen color. Burnt-orange has been used here.*

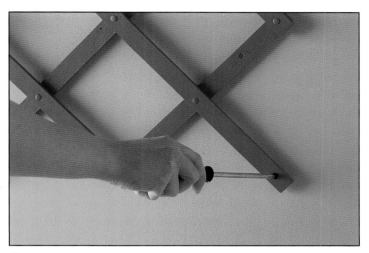

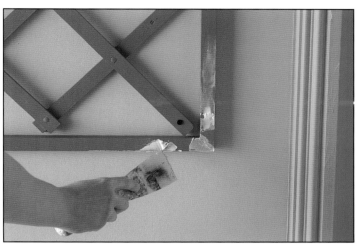

four *Drill holes in the wall with a masonry bit and insert plastic anchors. Drill pilot holes in the trellis slightly smaller than the screws, to prevent the wood from splitting, and then screw the trellis to the wall.*

five *Attach the frame around the trellis by screwing it onto the wall. Fill and paint over the tops of the screws and any gaps. When the trellis and frame are dry, give the whole hanging rack a second coat of paint.*

DECORATIVE CIRCLES

THERE IS NO REASON why the papers used for the walls and roofs of dolls' houses cannot be used on a full-sized wall. You could confine them to a limited area, such as below a chair-rail or within paneling, or use them more extensively all over the wall. Here, the wall has been painted a complementary color to the paper's and then circles have been cut out of the paper to reveal the color behind.

YOU WILL NEED

scrap paper

pencil

colored pencil

doll's house paper

latex paint for the base color

paint roller

paint-mixing tray

round template

craft knife

self-healing cutting mat

long metal ruler

wallpaper paste

pasting brush

clear varnish

varnish brush

one *Plan and draw the whole design to scale on paper. Choose a paper with a small repeat pattern for the circles. Choose your base-paint color to coordinate with the paper; it may help to paint swatches on scrap paper to see how well the colors work together.*

two *Paint the wall in the base color. Decide on the size of the circles; you may have a plate, saucer or other round object of the right size, which you can use as a template. Decide on the spacing of the circles.*

three *Trim the paper, ready for pasting, using a craft knife on a cutting mat. Cut out the circles. Paste the paper to the wall as if it were wallpaper. Be especially careful of the edges where you have cut out circles, as these are delicate. If you prefer, draw guidelines for positioning the cut-out circles; otherwise, position them by eye. When the paste is completely dry, apply two coats of clear varnish, letting it dry between coats.*

PULL-DOWN STOOL

RESTRICTED SPACE IN APARTMENTS is common; you need to use every inch of space, and it is not easy to fit in extra seating, by the telephone in the hall for example, or in any other small area. Folding chairs are an obvious solution, but the problem of where to store them still arises. One answer is to adapt the clever folding brackets and hinges available from do-it-yourself stores, which are usually used for tables and shelves, to make a folding stool. Instead of a solid piece of fiberboard, you could use dowel decking, such as that used in bathrooms. It is important that the stool is attached to a masonry wall and not to a partition wall, which will not be able to take the weight, resulting in damage to the wall and person on the stool. Check the manufacturer's recommendations for fitting the right kind of screws and plugs.

YOU WILL NEED

pair of folding brackets with screws

silver spray paint

medium-density fiberboard

saw

pencil

ruler

compass or circular templates in three sizes

clamp

drill, with wood and masonry bits

jigsaw (optional)

medium-grade sandpaper

paintbrush

yellow paint

clear varnish or lacquer

screwdriver

2 long screws and plastic anchors

level

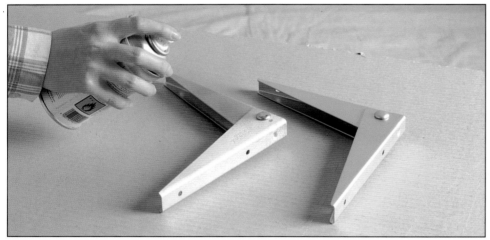

one *Spray the brackets silver on a protected work surface.*

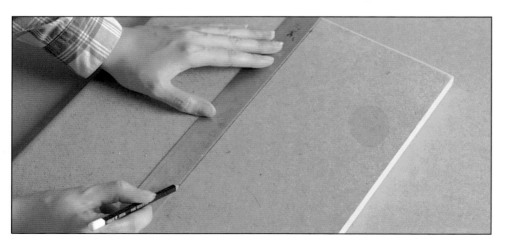

two *Cut the fiberboard to the right size for the seat: 12–18 x 8 inches is normal. Draw a line down the center of the seat.*

three *Place the brackets on the seat and mark their positions in pencil.*

four *With the compass, draw three circles of increasing size. Alternatively, find three circular objects of suitable sizes to use as templates.*

five *Holding the seat firmly clamped to the work bench, drill a ring of holes just inside the pencil marks; this will allow you to cut out the circles with a jigsaw. If you are not confident with a jigsaw, take the seat to a hardware store or an employee at a lumberyard who will cut the holes for you.*

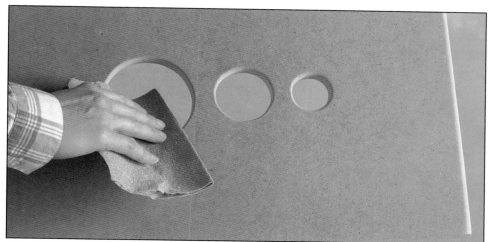

six *Sand the holes to a smooth finish, both inside and on the top and bottom.*

seven *Sand off any pencil marks or fingerprints to prepare the surfaces for painting.*

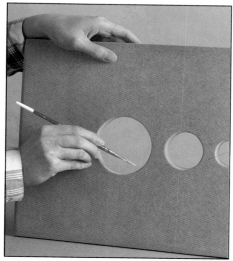

eight *Paint the inside of the holes yellow to highlight them.*

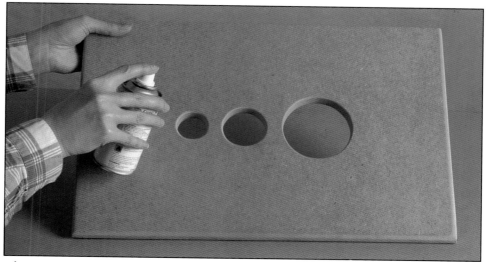

nine *Seal the seat with clear varnish or lacquer. A spray type is easy to use and will give a smooth finish.*

CONTINUED OVER ➤

ten *Screw the brackets to the seat. Hold the seat against the wall, which must be a masonry wall, and mark the position of the first hole with a pencil.*

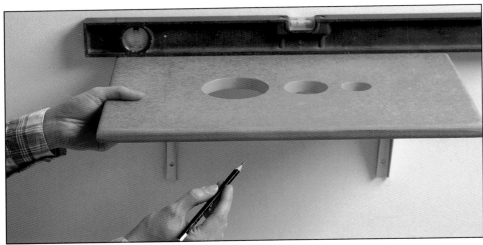

eleven *Drill a hole using the masonry bit. Insert the plastic anchor and screw the seat loosely to the wall. Level the seat using a level and mark the position for the second hole on the wall. Drill the hole, insert the plastic anchor and screw the other side of the seat to the wall.*

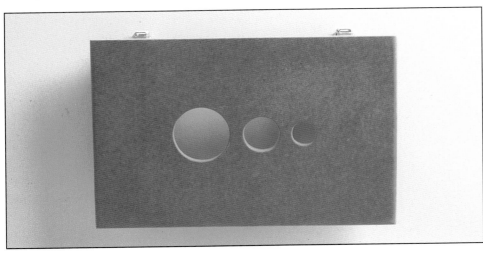

twelve *Check that the stool folds neatly against the wall.*

LOUNGE CHAIR

LOUNGE CHAIRS COME IN various heights and with all kinds of additional features, but the fabrics, which are mostly garish prints and stripes, seem at odds with the stylish tubular frames. Apart from the obvious solution of re-covering, using the existing fabric as a pattern, a clever alternative is to make a textural webbing cover. This fabric is long-lasting and overcomes the problem of sagging. Re-covered in this way, the lounge chair offers both comfort and durability.

YOU WILL NEED

lounge chair

chrome cleaner

soft cloth

tape measure

16 yards upholstery webbing rolls

masking tape

pencil

scissors

needle

matching thread

6 packets large eyelets

hammer

softwood block

6½ yards cord or rope

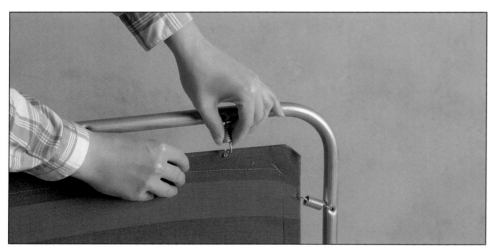

one *Remove and discard the old cover. Thoroughly clean the metal frame with chrome cleaner and a soft cloth. Measure the width of the frame for the horizontal straps, and almost double this measurement so that the ends of the straps will very nearly meet in the middle.*

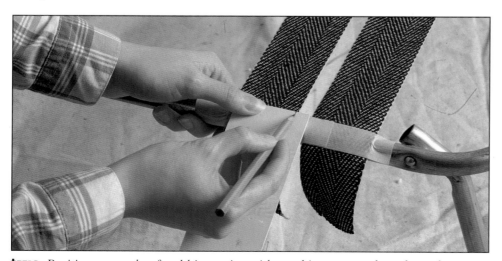

two *Position a couple of webbing strips with masking tape and work out how many strips you will need in each section of the frame. Cut the webbing to length and hem the ends.*

three *Follow the manufacturer's instructions for applying an eyelet to each end of the straps.*

four *Turn the lounge chair upside down, wrap the straps around the frame and fasten the ends together with cord or rope where they meet in the middle. Leave a gap wide enough for another strap near the hinges of the lounge chair.*

five *Starting at the foot, secure a vertical strap with an eyelet. Weave the strap under and over the double thickness of the horizontal straps until you reach the top. Secure the end with another eyelet.*

six *Near the hinges, thread another horizontal strap through the vertical ones, but wrap the ends around the two outermost verticals instead of around the frame.*

Kitchens

KITCHENS ARE THE HEART of any home. So why not make yours look like it? You can, but remember—behind every outstanding kitchen is an outstanding decorator, for this is one room in the house where combining fun and function without breaking the bank requires ingenuity, and lots of it.

Look at what the kitchen has to be: work room, family room, storage room, dining room. Achieving all that in a functional, flexible, minimal-maintenance room AND making it a place where people like to be, depends on careful planning and lots of clever ideas.

The projects in this chapter present some of these ideas, many of which bring a new meaning to the word "recycling." The kitchen is where discarded objects come into their own—they not only look great but have a useful purpose as well.

The next time you visit a fruitstand collect some fruit crates—with a coat of paint and a length of ribbon they make great stackable storage boxes. Transform a flea market window box into a striking and practical shelf for bottles, or suspend three metal garden sieves on lengths of chain to create a vegetable rack that's just striking. There's also a horticultural solution for the windows. To flood the kitchen with warm, glowing

In any kitchen it is essential to be able to find the silverware, and a decorative silverware box in a striking modern design is a real asset.

light, yet not with the stares of passers-by, try our wonderful blind made from a length of scrim edged with broad strips of burlap. With its cotton-reel pulleys it sounds kind of old-fashioned, but that only adds to its appeal.

Once you've seen how much can be done with so little, your imagination will take over and no object, corner or surface will escape your attention. Your kitchen won't just be a better place to work, but bright and cheerful enough to make your whole day.

COUNTRY-STYLE SHELF

THE HEART HAS BEEN USED to convey a universal message in folklore for centuries. Here, a heart has been used to make a stamp that resembles a four-leafed clover. The smaller heart is a traditional solid shape that fits neatly along the edges of the shelf supports. The background color was applied in three separate coats and rubbed back slightly between coats; a final lighter color was applied over the top. When the shelf was dry, it was sanded with medium-grade sandpaper to reveal some of the grain and layers of color.

YOU WILL NEED

tracing paper

pencil

spray adhesive

high-density foam, such as uhholstery foam

scalpel

deep red latex paint

plate

paintbrush

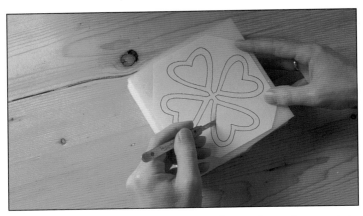

one *Trace and transfer the pattern shapes from the template section. Lightly spray the shapes with adhesive and place them on the foam. Cut around the outline of the shapes with a scalpel. Cut out the single heart shape. First cut out the outline, then part the foam and cut all the way through.*

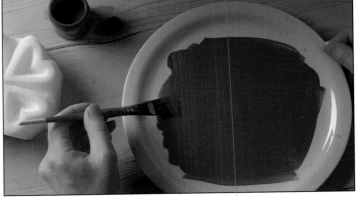

two *Use the stamp as a measuring guide to estimate the number of prints that will fit along the back of the shelf. Mark their position with a pencil. Spread an even coating of deep red paint on a plate.*

three *Make a test print of the clover-leaf stamp on a scrap of paper to ensure that the stamp is not overloaded with paint. Referring to the pencil guidelines, press the stamp into the paint and make the first print on the wood.*

four *Continue until you have completed all of the clover-leaf shapes. Try not to get the finish too even; this is a rustic piece of furniture. Finish off the shelf with a row of small hearts along the support edges, then add one between each large motif.*

MEDITERRANEAN CRATES

WOODEN FRUIT AND VEGETABLE crates are much too good to be thrown away once their original contents have been used up, so rescue them from your local market and dress them up with color and ribbon to make a great set of useful containers. The crates here work especially well, as they have a base that can be separated and used as a lid. These rustic Mediterranean crates look wonderful stacked with candles, tablecloths or other bright odds and ends.

YOU WILL NEED

3 wooden fruit or vegetable crates

sandpaper

pliers

wire cutters

staple gun (optional)

powder paint: red, blue and green

paintbrushes

40 inches checked ribbon

scissors

one *Rub off any rough edges on the crates with sandpaper. Detach the base from one of them to be the "lid." Remove and replace any protruding staples if necessary.*

two *Mix the powder paints according to the manufacturer's instructions. Paint one of the crates red on the inside, blue on the outside, and green along the top edges.*

three *Paint the other crate green on the inside, red along the top edges and blue on the outside.*

four *Paint the lid blue. Bind the six center joints with crosses of checked ribbon, tied securely at the back.*

WINDOW BOX SHELF

THIS ROUGH-HEWN RUSTIC box, stained dark brown, was found at an antique store, and was probably in a garden shed thirty years ago. It is a good reminder not to write anything off until you have assessed its potential, for here, painted and refurbished, it is both decorative and useful. Hang a window box on your kitchen wall to hold all the colorful bottles and jars that are usually hidden in a cupboard.

YOU WILL NEED

wooden window box

sandpaper

latex paint: red, blue, green and white

paintbrushes

fine-grade steel wool

shellac button polish

drill, with wood bit

2 plastic anchors and screws

screwdriver

one *Rub down the wooden surface of the window box with sandpaper. Paint it in bright colors, highlighting different parts in contrasting colors. Let dry.*

two *Mix white paint with water in equal parts and apply a coat of this all over the window box. Let dry. Rub back the white paint with fine-grade steel wool so that it just clings to the wood grain and imperfections.*

three *Apply a coat of button polish to protect the surface from stains and to improve the aged effect. Drill two holes in the back of the window box and attach it to the kitchen wall.*

HANGING JAM JARS

THIS BRIGHT IDEA FOR getting double mileage out of kitchen shelves is borrowed from a tool shed. Woodworkers and gardeners line the undersides of their shelves with jam jar lids and then screw in jars filled with nuts, bolts, nails, screws and other useful things. Everything is kept neat, in view and within easy reach. Fill your jars with cookies, candy, rice or different types of beans and lentils. You could even use smaller jars to create an unusual and inexpensive herb and spice rack.

YOU WILL NEED

4 or more jam jars, with lids

kitchen shelf

pencil

awl

screws (no longer than the shelf depth)

screwdriver

one *Arrange the jam jar lids along the underside of the shelf. There should be sufficient room between them for a hand to fit and sufficient depth for the jars to fit. Lightly mark the positions with a pencil.*

two *Use an awl to make two holes through each lid into the shelf.*

three *Screw the lids securely in place.*

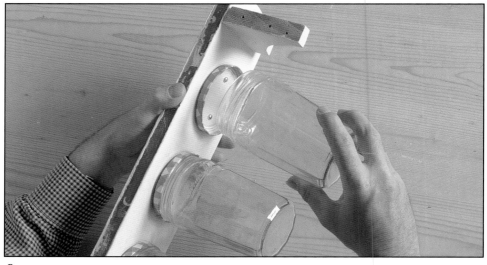

four *Screw on the jars. It is easier to do this with the shelf on a work surface than with the shelf already hanging on the wall. Hang up the shelf.*

eight *Clip the three top chain lengths together with a combine hook and add an additional length to suspend the rack from the ceiling. Find a beam for the ceiling hook, as it needs to be strong to support the weight of vegetables.*

Above: The vegetable rack will look equally at home in a rustic interior or a stark, modern one.

COLORFUL KITCHEN CHAIR

INTRODUCE PROVENÇAL CHECKS and stripes to the kitchen with soft furnishings; many kitchen chairs have detachable pads or padded seats, and the informality of the kitchen perfectly suits a mix of frills, ties and prints. Consider the colors and patterns of your tablecloths and then, using bright colors, simple ginghams or stripes, mix and match. As an alternative, smart ticking stripes or pale pastels would give this old-fashioned chair a sophisticated air.

YOU WILL NEED
kitchen chair
tissue or pattern-cutting paper
pencil
thin foam
scissors
3 yards of 54-inch fabric
fabric marker
tape measure
ruler or triangle
dressmaker's pins
sewing machine
matching thread
iron
ribbons or ties (optional)

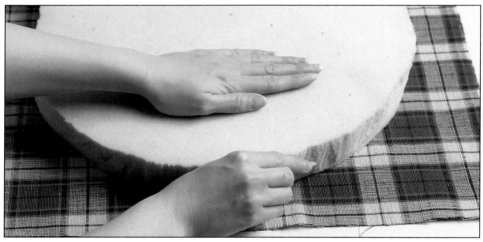

one *Using the thin paper, draw the shape of the chair seat and cut it out of foam to form a cushion. On the wrong side of the fabric, draw the cushion shape again, adding a ¾-inch seam allowance all around. Measure the depth and the circumference of the foam.*

two *Cut a bias strip of fabric to these measurements, with a 1½-inch seam allowance all around. Attach the strip to the seat cover, by pinning and machine-stitching the pieces together all around the edge, with right sides together.*

three *Decide how deep you want the skirt to be. The length is three times the circumference of the seat.*

four *From straight-grain fabric, cut one continuous panel or join two together. Hem the bottom edge and the two ends. Fold, pin and press the fabric into box pleats. When pleated, the skirt should be the same length as the sides and front of the cushion pad. Sew along the top edge to secure the pleats. Attach the pleats to the bias-cut strip of the chair cover, with right sides together. Leave the back edge of the chair cover free of pleats, but turn up the hem allowance on the bias strip.*

five *Stitch ribbons or ties to the unfrilled edge and tie them around the backrest to hold the cover in place. Alternatively, cut ties from leftover fabric. Machine-stitch them with right sides together, leaving a small gap. Trim the seam allowances and clip the corners. Turn the ties right side out through the gap and slip-stitch the gap closed. Attach the self-ties in the same way as the ribbons.*

CUT-ABOVE TILES

IF YOU'D LIKE TO RETILE your kitchen but are short on funds, this is the cheapest way of achieving the effect: simple photocopies cut into tile shapes, pasted to the wall and then varnished for protection. Find an appropriate motif that will fit neatly into a tile shape. Then you just need enough patience to cut out and paste the copies onto the wall. You could adapt the idea to other areas of the house: just change the motif to fit.

YOU WILL NEED
cutlery motifs
pencil
metal ruler
craft knife
self-healing cutting mat
straightedge
level
wallpaper paste
pasting brush
clear varnish
varnish brush

one *Photocopy the motif as many times as necessary. Draw a tile-shaped outline around the photocopies. Carefully cut the photocopies to the shape and size of a tile using the craft knife and cutting mat.*

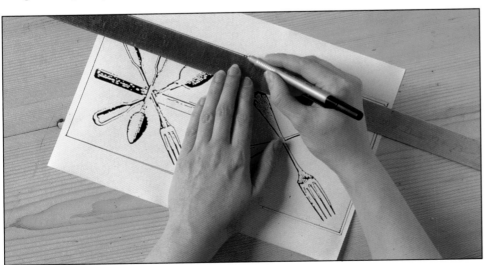

two *Using a straightedge and level, draw guidelines for positioning the tiles on the wall to make sure you put the photocopies on straight. Paste the photocopies onto the wall, making sure you cover all the guidelines. Let dry.*

three *Several coats of varnish will protect the wall and create a wipeable finish. Let dry between coats.*

CUTLERY BOX

THIS PROJECT FUSES THE clarity of high-tech design with the starkness of surrealist sculpture—and provides an ideal place to keep your cutlery at the same time. The stylish boxes look especially good in a modern kitchen, where chrome and stainless steel keep the lines crisp and the surfaces reflective. Make separate boxes for knives, forks and spoons and say goodbye forever to rummaging in the kitchen drawer.

YOU WILL NEED
small silver-plated knife, fork and spoon, polished
3 metal boxes with lids
felt-tipped pen
coarse-grade sandpaper
metal file
metal-bonding compound (Chemical Metal)
craft knife

one *Bend the knife to a right angle halfway along the handle, over the edge of a table if necessary. Mark the position of the knife on the box. Roughen the parts of the knife and the box that will touch, with sandpaper and a file respectively.*

two *Mix the metal-bonding compound. Follow the manufacturer's instructions. Apply to the roughened area on the lid. The knife will be attached at this point, so the bond must be strong.*

three *Press the knife handle into position on the bonding. Use a fine instrument, such as a craft knife, to remove any excess bonding. Repeat these steps for the fork and spoon and their two metal boxes.*

TROMPE-L'OEIL LINOLEUM

LINOLEUM NOW COMES in many thicknesses, colors and patterns, and while it doesn't quite have the appeal of a beautiful classical floor, by cutting it into "three-dimensional" patterns and playing with slight color variations you can create stunning effects. Aside from the fact that linoleum is durable, water-resistant and probably one of the least expensive floor coverings, given this dramatic treatment, it can become the centerpiece of any kitchen. Rolls of linoleum and floor adhesive were used in this project, but you could also use self-glued tiles to make a floor reminiscent of a Venetian palazzo.

YOU WILL NEED

power sander, with fine-grade sandpaper

tape measure

pencil

paper

ruler

long metal ruler or straightedge

hardboard sheet

saw

linoleum rolls in different colors

craft knife

contact floor adhesive

one *You need a smooth, flat surface. If necessary, lay a marine-plywood or hardwood floor. Make sure that no nail heads are exposed, then lightly sand the floor.*

two *Measure the floor. To ensure a good fit, it's very important to work out the pattern on paper first, using the template.*

◄

three *Draw grid lines on the floor as a guide for laying the linoleum shapes. Draw each of the pattern shapes on a piece of hardboard and cut them out with a saw.*

four *Cut out the linoleum around the templates. Accuracy is important.*

five *Try out your pattern in pieces of linoleum and see if any need trimming. Number them on the back to fit them together more easily. Use contact adhesive to glue the tiles to the floor.*

VERMEER-STYLE MARBLE

YOU MAY BE FACED WITH a hardboard floor and long for the grandeur and impact of a marble one. Marbling is relatively easy to do. A wonderfully strong pattern is used here, taken from Vermeer's Old Master paintings. You may choose to do a simple checkerboard or even pretend you have a huge slab of marble. Find a small piece of marble as reference (from the great variety of marbles to choose from) to create a realistic effect. This technique is not suitable for anywhere where there is a lot of moisture, but in the right place it can look amazing.

YOU WILL NEED

tape measure
paper
pencil
ruler
black felt-tipped pen
white undercoat paint
paint roller
long straightedge, e.g. skirting length
artist's oil colors: black, light gray, dark gray, and silver
oil-based glaze
paintbrushes
lint-free cloth
bird's feather or quill
softening brush
dry cloth
fine artist's brush
turpentine
black oil-based eggshell paint
matte varnish

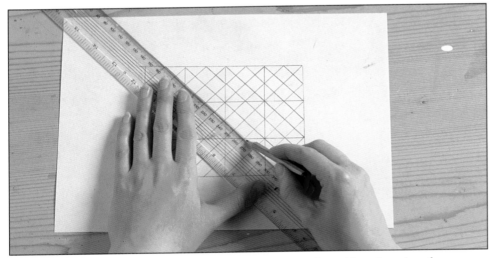

one *Measure your room, then draw a scale plan and a grid on it, using the template at the back of the book.*

two *Fill in your design, starting from the middle point of the floor plan and working out to the edges.*

three *You need a very flat surface, such as hardboard or marine-plywood. Undercoat the floor with a couple of coats of white paint.*

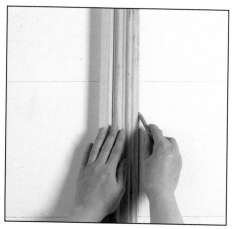

four *Draw the design on the floor in pencil. Put a small dab of black paint in each square that is going to be painted black.*

five *Add a little light gray oil paint to the oil-based glaze and apply it very thinly with a brush to all the squares that do not have black dots and will therefore be white "marble."*

six *With a lint-free cloth, soften the glaze while it is still wet to blend it and remove all traces of brush marks.*

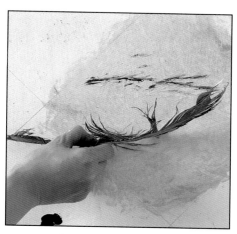

seven *Dip a bird's feather or quill into a mixture of black paint thinned with a little oil-based glaze, and gently draw across the surface, to simulate the veins of the marble.*

eight *Use the softening brush to blur the outlines of the veining and blend them with the background. Wipe the brush regularly on a dry cloth to avoid smudges.*

nine *With a fine artist's brush, further soften the effect by adding turpentine, which will dissipate the lines. You can also add more of the same color or a second color, but remember to soften it again.*

CONTINUED OVER ➤

ten *Clean up the edges of the pencil squares with the corner of a dry cloth.*

eleven *Carefully fill in the black squares indicated by the black dots.*

twelve *Using a little dark gray or silver paint, applied directly onto a brush dampened with turpentine, soften the black in swirling motions so that it looks like slate. Finally, give the floor several coats of varnish.*

WOODEN MESSAGE BOARD

A MESSAGE BOARD IS AN essential piece of equipment in a family kitchen and can also be an attractive display unit. This one makes a pleasant change from the utilitarian and unappealing cork type. Using a darker shade on the wooden strips and a lighter tone of the same color on the wall produces a coordinated look. The slats used here are 1 x 1 inch, but you could use a different size if desired.

YOU WILL NEED
tape measure
wooden slats
pencil
saw
blue-green latex paint
paintbrush
level
straightedge
drill, with masonry and
wood bits
plastic anchors
wood screws and screwdriver
small nails
hammer
bulldog clips

one *Measure the wood to the correct length and cut as many pieces as you will need. Paint the wood with latex paint.*

two *Mark guidelines for attaching the slats using the level and straightedge. Drill holes and insert plastic anchors. Drill holes in the slats and screw them to the wall.*

three *Tap in nails at intervals along the slats. Hang the clips from the nails.*

ON THE SHELF

EVERYONE HAS SHELVES somewhere in the home, but how many of us have thought of decorating them with different styles of edging? This project includes three different designs using natural materials that would be suitable for a kitchen. Experiment with anything and everything around the home, and you'll be surprised at just how innovative and exciting shelf edging can be. If you attach your trimmings with double-sided tape, they can be removed in an instant so, with very little effort, you can change the designs as often as you like.

YOU WILL NEED

tape measure

string

scissors

tape

red raffia

Chinese-language newspaper

pencil

double-sided tape or pins

one *Measure the length of your shelf. Cut a piece of string about 2 inches longer than the shelf, so it can turn around the corners. Cut more lengths of string, approximately 6–8 inches long.*

two *Gather together bunches of about three lengths of string. Fold the bunches into loops and then pass the ends over the string and through the center of the loop. Pull the loops taut to secure them. You can tape the string to the work surface if it makes it easier to work on it. Cut small pieces of red raffia and tie them into small knots between every two or three strands of looped string. Cut the raffia close to the knot.*

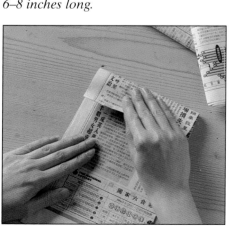

three *For the newspaper edging, measure the shelf. Cut strips the length of the shelf, and the depth you require. Fold each strip, accordion-fashion.*

four *Experiment by drawing different designs onto each folded strip. Cut out the edging shapes. Open them out and smooth them flat. Choose the shape that co-ordinates best with the style of decoration in the kitchen or reflects the shapes of the contents of the shelves.*

five *For the raffia edging, cut a piece of raffia the length of the shelf. Cut many short lengths of raffia.*

six *Loop them singly onto the main piece, as for the string edging. Tighten the loops and fill in any gaps. Trim the ends to one length to make an even fringe. Use double-sided tape or pins to attach the trimmings to the edge of each shelf.*

Tuscan Doorway

WITH PATIENCE AND A little confidence, you can attempt a simple *trompe-l'oeil* wall decoration to create the atmosphere of a Tuscan country house in your own kitchen. The key to this rustic look is to layer the colors and then rub the layers back to reveal those underneath. The rest of the effect is created by masking off successive areas and finally adding simple, freehand "coach lines," so called because they are similar to the decorative lines on the liveries on horse-drawn coaches. It doesn't matter if your lines aren't perfect; it adds to the look. A final wash of watery ocher enhances the aged look.

one *Experiment with colors. You can pick quite strong shades, as they will soften when they are sanded back. Apply the cream base coat.*

two *Wash over the base coat with a warm yellow paint.*

three *Draw your design to scale on paper using a triangle or ruler.*

four *Measure and draw the straight lines on the wall, using the level and straightedge.*

five *Draw the curve, using a pencil tied to a length of string in the same way as you would use a compass.*

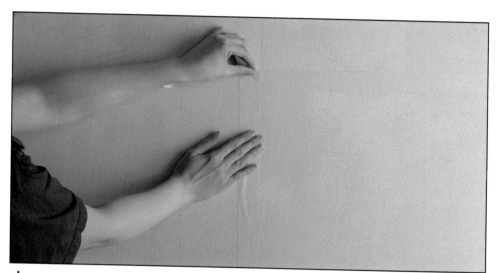

six *Mask off the areas to be painted in terra-cotta with tape.*

seven *Paint in the terra-cotta areas and immediately remove the tape.*

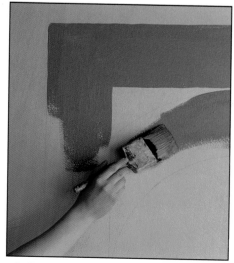

eight *Paint the other areas green, masking off if necessary.*

nine *Paint a thin cream outline around all the edges by hand.*

CONTINUED OVER ➤

ten *Lightly sand over the design, going back to the base coat in some areas and leaving others untouched.*

eleven *Wash over everything again with the warm yellow paint. Mask off the squares in the border. Paint the outlines and immediately remove the tape.*

twelve *Paint in all the outlines and immediately remove the tape.*

thirteen *Use the brown pencil to draw in extra-fine lines in the semi-circular "fan-light."*

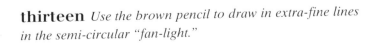

PAINTED BRICK "TILES"

THIN BRICK TILES ARE widely available and take on a new character when painted an interesting color. You can arrange them in traditional brick-fashion or one above the other. Herringbone and basketweave patterns are also possible. As the right side is rough and the back is smooth, you can also have fun making patterns with the textures. Halved and quartered bricks make interesting borders and more complex variations on whole-brick designs. The color you paint the bricks is all-important; the same design in white looks very different from ocher, for example.

YOU WILL NEED

straightedge
level
pencil
thin bricks
brick adhesive
hacksaw
pale yellow latex paint
paintbrush
grout (optional)

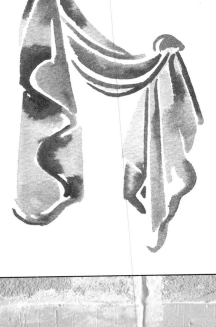

one *Use the straightedge and level to draw guidelines for the positions of the bricks on the wall. Then, using adhesive and following the brick manufacturer's instructions, stick the bricks in place. Cut some bricks in half or in quarters with the hacksaw. Use the smaller pieces to make a border at chair-rail height.*

two *Give the bricks a first coat of latex paint.*

three *If you wish, grout the bricks and then paint over them and grout again. Otherwise, just give the bricks a second coat of paint.*

BURLAP & SCRIM BLINDS

THE NATURAL MATERIALS OF burlap and linen scrim are teamed up with bamboo canes to make this unusual Roman blind. The blind obscures the window effectively at night, and by day the sunlight streams through the scrim, making it appear almost transparent. The bamboo canes give the window a "potting shed" effect, and the ingenious pulley adds a distinctive touch—not only does it look interesting, it is also practical.

YOU WILL NEED

burlap, to fit window

scissors

scrim, same size as burlap

stapler

6 bamboo canes

iron

tape measure

saw

iron-on hem tape (optional)

needle

matching sewing thread

¾-inch brass rings

¾-inch hinged rings

coat hangers

pliers

pencil

thin cardboard

4 empty wooden spools

4 screws

screwdriver

washers (optional)

string

one *Cut the burlap into four strips. Working on the sides first, fold a strip of burlap down the length of either side of the scrim to form a border, and staple the burlap and scrim together.*

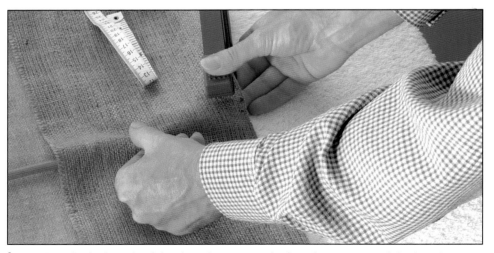

two *Divide the length of the drop by six to calculate the position of the bamboo canes. Saw the bamboo canes to fit the width of the window. Insert the first cane in position by holding it with the ends pushed up into the burlap border and stapling either side of it to make a channel. Repeat this process on the other side. Position the remaining canes in the same way, at equal intervals.*

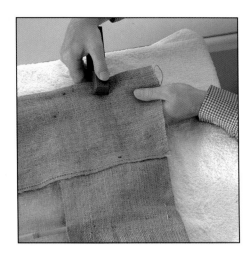

◄ **three** *Fold the burlap over the scrim at the bottom, as you did with the side, with a bamboo cane along its bottom fold. Staple this in place. Repeat this process with the top edge.*

four *If you are using iron-on hem tape, place it under the seam between the scrim and burlap and press it with a hot iron.* ➤

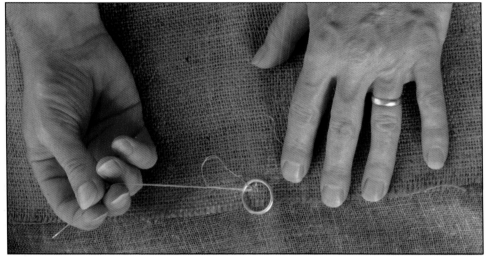

five *Stitch a brass ring to every point at which the burlap and scrim meet on a bamboo strut, including the bottom strut. Take the needle right through the fabric so that the thread goes around the bamboo each time for a strong attachment. Sew the two hinged rings, in line with the others, on either side of the blind top.*

six *Trim off overlapping burlap. If the fabric frays, insert some iron-on hem tape.*

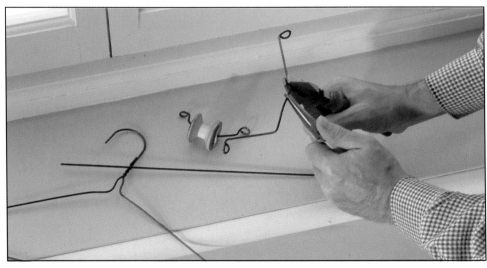

seven *Cut five lengths of coat hanger wire from the longest part of the hanger—three lengths at 6¼ inches and two lengths at 10 inches.*

eight *Using the photograph as a guide, draw the shape to hold the spools onto a piece of cardboard. Then bend the shorter pieces of wire to that shape so that they will hold the spools.*

CONTINUED OVER ➤

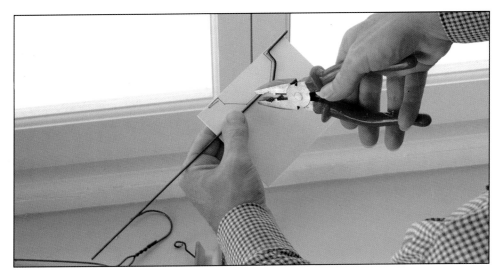

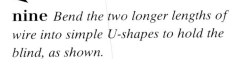

nine *Bend the two longer lengths of wire into simple U-shapes to hold the blind, as shown.*

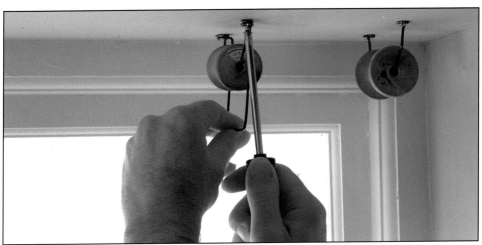

ten *Screw the first spool into the top right corner. Ensure that the screw heads are big enough, or add a washer to get a firm attachment. Align the loops of a pulley and a longer wire and attach both gadgets in place with the same screws. Screw the other spool and wire on the other side of the window, the same distance from the edge.*

eleven *Open out the hinged ring and use it to clip the blind up in position in the window.*

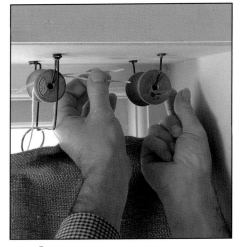

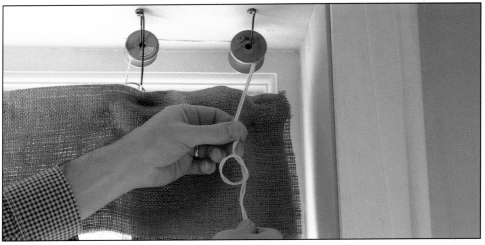

twelve *To thread the blind, start at the bottom and tie the string to the lowest ring. Thread up through the rings and over the pulleys. Do the same for both sets of rings.*

thirteen *Tie the two strings together about 6 inches down from the corner pulley to prevent the blind from pulling up unevenly. Screw the last cotton spool into the wall for tying the string when you pull the blind.*

SHEET-METAL TREAD MATS

SHEET-METAL TREAD MATS are a versatile and hard-wearing floor covering and will give a room a unique look. They may be painted—either plain or patterned—but also look absolutely dazzling left in their natural state. The sheets come in a wide range of metals, including copper, zinc and stainless steel, and can be cut to size. Lay the sheets on concrete or a subfloor of hardboard, chipboard or marine-plywood.

YOU WILL NEED

sheet-metal tread mats

wood scrap

metal file

drill, with metal pilot drill bit, and wood drill bit (optional)

wood screws (optional)

screwdriver

floor adhesive (optional)

metal or wooden quadrant beading

one *Use a metal file to file away any rough edges, but be careful not to create file marks on the visible top surface of the sheets. Use a small piece of wood as a rest and a metal pilot drill bit to drill holes in every corner of the mats and at intervals of 8 inches along all the sides, depending on the size of the sheets.*

two *If you are laying the metal sheets over wooden floor boards, you can screw through the holes in the metal directly into the wood surface with wood screws.*

three *Butt up the sheets together and continue screwing them to the floor. If you have a concrete floor, the metal sheets can be glued directly in place. To finish, fit metal or wooden quadrant beading around the edges.*

BEDROOMS

IT DOESN'T MATTER WHETHER your fantasies run to the exotic, the minimal or the regal, the bedroom is one room in the house where you can indulge youself to your heart's content. After all, it's your room, so you can do what you like.

Whatever your tastes, our ideas rely more on imagination than money, more on practical inspirations than complicated equipment. And with our shortcuts and great tips, decorating your bedroom won't put you to sleep. A good place to start is with the curtains. Tip number one: Forget about curtain or fabric stores. Instead, try a specialty sari store. As soon as you enter you will be enveloped in colors you've only dreamed about. Imagine sunlight filtering through a window dressed with gossamer-light, deep-hued saris, the lightest breeze creating shivers of movement among the golden threads.

Or perhaps you dream of a bedroom of cool serenity and creative order. This calls for Japanese inspiration: simple, uncluttered lines, plain fabrics and pale colors. A garden trellis covered with heavy tracing paper becomes a translucent screen, providing privacy with the softest light—the perfect solution for windows that open onto a blank wall.

A bed draped in cool white cotton adds romance and grandeur to any bedroom. It is simple and easy to create.

Once again, side-step traditional stores and head straight to a painter's supplier—decorator's dust-sheets are incredibly inexpensive and make a perfect covering for a futon mattress. Making the base is easier than you think. To cast a subtle light on your Asian dreams, make a bedside lamp from corrugated cardboard and bamboo skewers.

Sleep like a king or queen under a faux-carved bed with a canopy. Store-bought decorative wooden and plaster moldings provide the fanciful trimmings and the gilded finishing touches, and the effect of filigree wall paneling can be created by using nothing more than simple radiator cover panels.

TRIPOD LIGHT

THIS CONTEMPORARY-LOOKING standard lamp appears quite delicate, but the tripod legs are very stable. The simple design makes it ideal for a Japanese-style room, particularly if a plain shade is used. The base consists of three pieces of wooden dowel fitted into angled holes drilled in a circle of wood. The frame of the shade is covered with butter-colored muslin. The lamp is assembled by screwing a lamp attachment to the wooden disc, over a central hole through which the cord passes.

YOU WILL NEED

dark oak wood stain

1-yard lengths wooden dowel

soft cloth

pencil

compass (optional)

square piece of wood

clamp

2 scraps wood

coping saw

drill, with twist bit

craft knife or scalpel

wood glue

tape measure

large cylindrical shade frame

dressmaker's scissors

3 yards unbleached butter-colored muslin

dressmaker's pins

rust-colored 4-ply yarn

darning needle

shade holder

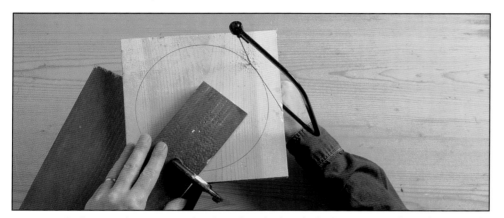

one *Rub the wood stain into the dowel with the cloth. Draw a circle with a 7-inch diameter on the square of wood, then clamp it ready for sawing. Protect it from the clamp with scraps of wood. Saw in from the edge at an angle and follow the curve with the blade. Move the wood around so that you can saw comfortably.*

two *Using a drill bit that is marginally narrower than the dowel, drill three angled holes through the wood circle. To do this, hold the drill directly above the center, then tilt it slightly toward the edge; the angle will then be correct.*

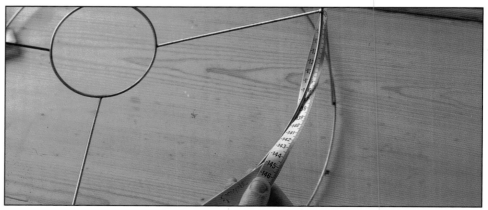

three *Shave the ends of the lengths of dowel slightly with a craft knife or scalpel, apply wood glue and then push them into the drilled holes. Apply glue to the lengths of dowel where they intersect. Let dry. To cover the frame, measure around the circumference and height. Cut a double thickness of muslin 4 inches wider than the height of the shade and long enough to fit around it, with an extra 1½ inches as a seam allowance. Pin one end of the muslin along a strut, leaving ¾ inch at each end for a seam, and gathering the fabric slightly as you go.*

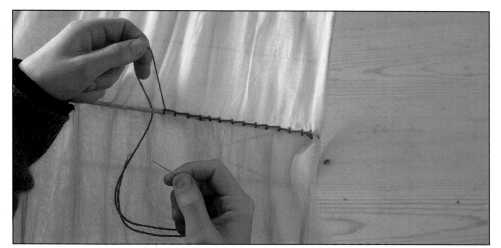

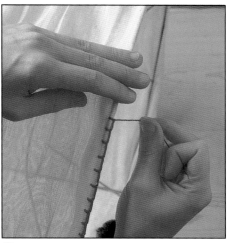

four *Pin the muslin along the next strut and sew in place using a blanket stitch. To sew a blanket stitch, insert the needle behind the strut and pull it out in front. Do not pull the yarn through. Take the needle through the loop of yarn, then pull the yarn tight. Continue stitching the muslin to each strut in the same way until you reach the first pinned seam. When you reach the final strut, join the two edges and stitch them together, still using blanket stitch.*

five *Finish off the top and bottom of the shade by rolling the edges around the wire frame, then pin and stitch them in place. Ask an electrician to attach the light attachments to the tripod, then place the shade on the holder.*

JAPANESE SCREEN

THIS SCREEN IS THE perfect treatment for a minimalist room scheme. It lets you hide from the outside world, yet you still benefit from the light filtering through. The screen is made from a simple wooden garden trellis, painted matte black, with heavyweight tracing paper stapled behind it. You can cut the trellis to fit your window recess, but always do it to the nearest square so it looks balanced.

YOU WILL NEED

garden trellis
blackboard paint
paintbrush
heavyweight tracing paper
staple gun
craft knife
red latex paint
drill, with wood bit
2 eyelets
tape measure
wire coat hanger
wire cutters
pliers
2 picture hooks

one *Paint the trellis black and let dry. Blackboard paint creates a perfectly matte finish, but other matte or gloss paints can be used. Staple sheets of tracing paper onto the back of the trellis. If necessary, trim the tracing paper with a craft knife so that no overlaps or seams are visible from the front. It must look like a single sheet.*

two *For added interest, paint one square red and let dry. Drill a very fine hole in the top of the trellis, at the first strut in from each end.*

three *Screw an eyelet into each hole. Measure the length of the window to determine how long the hooks for hanging should be. The base of the screen should touch the window frame below. Cut two pieces of coat-hanger wire to the correct length for the hooks, then hang the screen on these from picture-rail hooks.*

JAPANESE FUTON

THIS STYLISH AND UNCLUTTERED bedroom exudes a typically Japanese sense of simplicity, order and tranquility. Wooden pallets were used to make the bed base. These come in different sizes, but they can be sawn down and stacked to get the right size. The beautiful cream cotton bedcover is, unbelievably, a decorator's dust-sheet, decorated with knotted cords. Dust-sheets like this are incredibly cheap, so you can have the minimalist look for a minimal outlay. Just add a pillow and a cushion—and sleep well!

YOU WILL NEED

wooden pallets

medium- and fine-grade sandpaper

light-colored wood stain

paintbrush

2 yards black cotton cord

scissors

needle

thread

decorator's dust-sheet

2 black tassels

square cream-colored cushion

one *Rub down the wooden pallets, using first medium-grade, then fine-grade sandpaper. Apply a coat of light-colored wood stain to seal and color the wood. Lay the pallets on the floor to make a bed base.*

two *Cut six 12-inch lengths of black cotton cord. Make each length into a loop tied with a reef knot.*

three *Slip-stitch the knotted cords onto the dust-sheet to make three rows of two cords down the center of the bed. Spread the dust-sheet on the bed and fold it neatly over the pillows. Sew two black tassels onto the cushion and place it on the pillows. Tuck the dust-sheet under the mattress all the way around the bed.*

STAMPS AND DRY BRUSH

SOMETIMES, WITH A ROOM that has unusual furnishings, it is worthwhile giving it even more of a distinctive style, by making a design statement on the walls or floor. Here, the busy look of dry brushstrokes combines with the elegant simplicity of Japanese calligraphic characters. The result is a warm and uniquely stylish look that makes a memorable room.

YOU WILL NEED

calligraphy brush

ink: black and rust

white paper

scissors

paper glue

foam block

craft knife

hammer

masking tape

latex paint: cream, rust and white

large and small paint rollers

dry paintbrush

matte varnish

one *Paint your Japanese characters with the calligraphy brush first, following the examples shown in this project. Make photocopies of each design. Cut the characters out roughly and glue one of each character to the foam. Keeping the knife at an angle, cut off all the white paper and the foam underneath it, to make a raised stamp.*

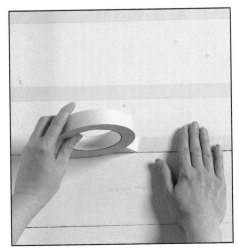

two *Prepare the floor, hammering in any protruding nails. Ensure that it is clean and dry. Tape off both edges of alternate boards. Apply a base coat of cream latex and let dry.*

three *Draw a dry brush, dipped into a little neat rust paint, across the unmasked boards in a series of parallel strokes, letting the base coat show through in places. Repeat this exercise with white paint, which softens the whole effect. Let dry, then repeat the procedure with both colors on the remaining boards.*

four *Plan your design of Japanese characters, using spare photocopies of the characters, roughly cut out. Using a small roller, ink some of the stamps with black ink. Replace some of the photocopies with black stamped characters.*

five *Repeat, using the rust-colored ink. Seal well with matte varnish and let dry.*

CHINESE LANTERN

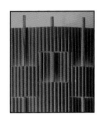

THIS STICK-AND-CARDBOARD lampshade has a natural look by day, but lights up like a skyscraper at night. Sheets of corrugated cardboard can be bought in a range of colors, from natural to fluorescent, and the wooden skewers can also be painted. You can use the lantern over any small table lamp or even a candle. If using a candle, place it in a secure holder.

YOU WILL NEED

metal ruler, approximately 1¼ inches wide

pen or pencil

13¾ x 10¼ inch sheet corrugated cardboard

scalpel

cutting mat

scrap paper

gold spray paint

package of wooden skewers

one *Use the width of the ruler as a spacer and draw vertical lines and slits across the cardboard. Cut slits across alternate columns, starting one in from the edge. Move the ruler down a width at a time; continue cutting to the bottom of the cardboard.*

two *Cut through the uncut rows in the same way, but starting with the ruler a half-drop down, so that the slits fall halfway between the first ones. Continue until the sheet is covered with a "brickwork" pattern of slits.*

three *Protect your work surface with scrap paper, then spray the smooth side of the cardboard with gold paint. Turn the cardboard over and weave the skewers in and out of the slits. Allow about 1 inch to protrude on one edge to give the shade legs to stand on. Trim the last column to within ½ inch of the slits so that the seam will not be too bulky. Overlapping the two edges (with the gold side inside), weave the last skewer through the double thickness to attach the lampshade edges together.*

CANOPY BED

THIS POSITIVELY REGAL CANOPY BED, draped with cool white cotton, will add majestic splendor to your bedroom. This sort of bed was popular around the second half of the nineteenth century, when fully draped four-posters became less fashionable. The style imitates the ornate four-poster, but is actually a box made to fit against the wall with a canopy that extends no more than a third of the length of the bed. This canopy is made out of a wood and picture-frame molding and adorned with plaster scrolls bought at a do-it-yourself store. The wall plaque is not strictly a part of the canopy, but it adds the finishing touch. Use a fine white fabric, such as voile, muslin or cotton sheeting, for the drapes.

YOU WILL NEED

plaster-cast head wall hanging

backing paper

shellac

paintbrushes

gold spray paint

black latex or poster paint

cloth

steel wool

2 scrolled plaster decorations

larger scrolled plaster decoration

62-inch fancy picture-frame molding

wood stain (optional)

2 x 1 inch strip wood, 46 inches long

62-inch door-frame molding

saw

mitering block

glue gun and glue sticks

3/4-inch wooden dowel, 4 inches long

curtain rings with clips

heavy-duty staple gun or eyelet screws

at least 11 yards fine white fabric

scissors

drill, with appropriate drill bit

plastic anchors

screwdriver and long screws

one *Place the plaster-cast head on a piece of backing paper to protect your work surface. Apply a coat of shellac to seal the surface. Let the first coat dry (for about 20 minutes), then apply a second coat of shellac. Let dry.*

two *Spray the head with gold spray paint. Let dry. Paint over the gold with black latex or poster paint. Cover the gold completely.*

three *Before the paint dries, rub most of it off using a slightly damp cloth. The black will have dulled the brassiness of the gold beneath.*

four *Burnish the high spots, such as the cheekbones, nose and brows, using steel wool. Give the scrolled decorations and picture-frame molding the same treatment, or stain them with your chosen color of wood stain. Cut the length of wood into one 30-inch and one 16-inch length. Cut the door-frame and picture-frame moldings into one 30-inch and two 16-inch lengths.*

five *Using a mitering block, saw the corners on the door-frame and picture-frame moldings that are to meet to make up the box shape. These will be both ends of the longest pieces and one end of each of the shorter ones.*

six *Glue the mitered door moldings at the edges and put the box shape together, placing the longest piece of wood at the back. Surround the front three sides with the fancy molding. Then glue the short piece of wood in the center of the piece as a reinforcement.*

seven *Cut the dowel into two 2-inch lengths and glue one piece into each top corner of the canopy at the back of the molding. They will act as supports for the scrolls.*

CONTINUED OVER ➤

eight *Apply hot glue to each length of dowel, and then stick the corner scroll decorations in place.*

nine *Attach the curtain rings with clips at equal distances around the inside of the moldings, using a heavy-duty staple gun or eyelet screws.*

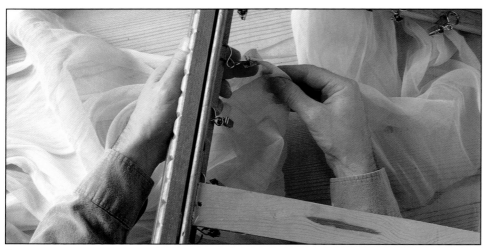

ten *Cut the fabric in half along its length. Before putting up the canopy, clip one length of fabric around one side to see how much fabric falls between each pair of clips. It will be easier to hang the drapes once the canopy is in place if you have worked out the spacing in advance. Remove the fabric. Attach the canopy to the wall near the ceiling, using appropriate attachments, and attach the plaster head to the wall. Clip the drapes in place and drape the fabric around the bed.*

GILDED CHAIR

MANY A BEAUTIFUL BENTWOOD chair is relegated to the attic because its cane seat is damaged. Re-caning is expensive and it is hard to find skilled craftsmen; it often seems easier and cheaper to buy a new chair. This is a shame because a bentwood chair can become the star of a room, with some effort but little expense, by setting in a solid seat. Once the cane has been removed, the chair looks wonderful with gold-leaf decoration.

YOU WILL NEED

wooden chair

craft knife

small screwdriver or awl

4 wooden blocks

pencil

saw

drill, with wood bit

8 wood screws

screwdriver

sheet of paper

scissors

sheet of plywood

masking tape

jigsaw (optional)

medium-grade sandpaper

size

paintbrush

gold leaf or two 25-sheet packages gold Dutch metal

clean, dry paintbrush

clean, dry cloth

varnish

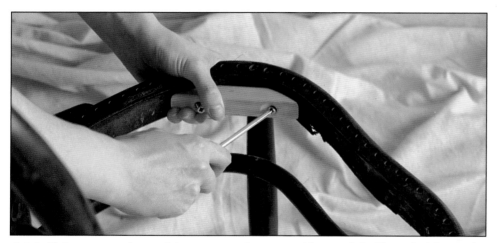

one *If the seat needs repairing, cut out the cane with a craft knife and pick out the remaining strands with a screwdriver or awl. To make the supporting corner blocks, hold the pieces of wood inside each corner, mark the shape on the wood and then cut the pieces to shape. Hold a corner block in position and drill through it into the chair. Screw the block into position. Repeat for all four corners.*

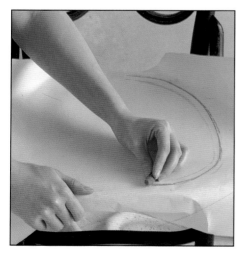

two *Lay the paper over the seat and trace the shape. Cut out to create the template. Tape the template to the plywood and draw around it.*

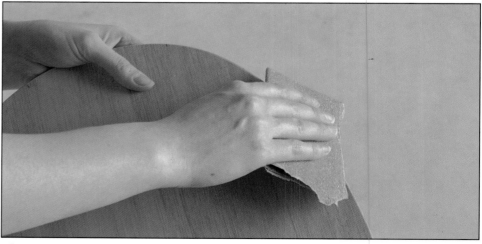

three *Cut around the pencil line. (A lumberyard can do this for you if you do not have a jigsaw.) Sand the edges of the wooden seat to fit and drop it into place. Prepare the chair for gilding by sanding all the surfaces lightly. Roughening the wood helps the size to adhere.*

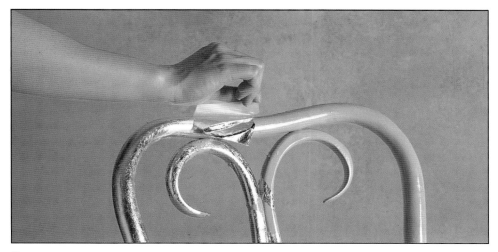 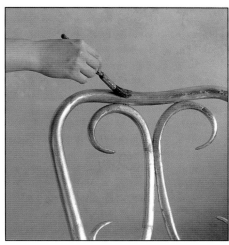

four *Paint the chair with size and let it dry. Follow the manufacturer's recommendations. Holding the gold leaf by the backing paper, lay a sheet on the chair. With a clean, dry brush, rub the gold leaf onto the chair. Continue until the chair is covered. It is very important that both the brush and your hands are clean and dry.*

five *Rub the chair with a clean, dry cloth to remove any loose flakes. Finally, to protect the gold leaf, seal the whole chair with varnish.*

GUSTAVIAN CHAIR

PRETTY GUSTAVIAN PAINTED CHAIRS give a lightness and elegance to bedroom furniture. They are expensive because few are available outside Scandinavia, where they originated. Create your own by painting a wooden chair of classic shape. It should have a padded seat, pretty outlines and enough space on the back rest for a motif. Traditional colors are grays, dark blues, aquamarine, honey yellow and red, as well as white.

YOU WILL NEED

classic wooden chair

medium- and fine-grade sandpaper

latex paint: white, blue-gray and black

household paintbrush

fine and medium paintbrushes

monogram motif

tracing paper

soft and hard pencils

masking tape

clear matte varnish

typeface or script samples (e.g. from a calligraphy book)

large sheet of paper

scissors

1 yard of 54-inch (or twice seat-cover width) white cotton fabric

indelible laundry or fabric marker

staple gun

needle

matching thread

gold and silver spray paint

one *Lightly sand the chair with medium-grade sandpaper to make a key for the paintwork. Paint the chair with an undercoat of white latex. Mix blue-gray latex then, using the fine paintbrush, carefully outline the shape of the back of the chair. Add similar detailing to the seat and legs. Let dry. Trace your chosen letters and scrolls. Turn the tracing paper over, and rub all over the back with the soft pencil. Turn it over, position it on the chair back and tape it in place. Go over the outlines with a hard pencil to transfer them to the chair.*

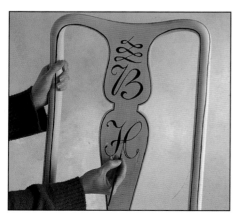

two *Fill in the outlines in blue-gray with the medium paintbrush. Refer to your original reference for where the brushstrokes should be thicker.*

three *Let dry. Apply a coat of matte varnish (water-based varnishes have very short drying times). Cut a piece of paper roughly the size of the chair seat pad, to give you an idea of the area to which you need to apply lettering. Photocopy type alphabets or sections of script, enlarging them, if necessary.*

four *Cut up the script and arrange the pieces on the paper. Put the paper against a brightly lit window, and smooth the fabric over the design. Attach to the glass with masking tape. Using the fabric marker, carefully trace over the letters. Cover the seat pad with the fabric, securing it on the back with staples. Take a second piece of fabric, just smaller than the underside of the seat, turn under the edges and sew in place to cover the staples.*

five *Lightly spray over the whole seat with gold paint. Repeat with silver. Replace the seat pad in the chair. Lightly sand the paint with fine-grade sandpaper to give it a charming, slightly aged effect.*

COPYCATS

CREATE A TRULY BEAUTIFUL setting by mixing fine, snowy-white linens, soft, filmy voile and crunchy tissue paper with gold lettering and initials. It looks extremely impressive and, although quite time-consuming, is easy to execute. Use any kind of calligraphy that appeals to you. (Here, the frontispiece from some sheet music was used.) Photocopy and enlarge your choice and trace it on to the voile, linen and tissue paper.

YOU WILL NEED

typeface or script samples (e.g. from a calligraphy book)

voile for curtain

masking tape

gold fabric paint

fine paintbrushes

iron

tissue paper

gold acrylic paint

organza ribbon

linen hand towel

carbon paper or soft pencil (optional)

hard pencil (optional)

one *Select different types of script samples. You may not find everything you need from one source, so look out for individual details. Photocopy the script samples, enlarging them to size. Experiment by moving the pieces of script around to create pleasing combinations and arrangements. Position the photocopies on the voile for the curtain, devising a pattern along its length.*

two *Tape your photocopy to a table or work surface, ensuring that it is flat. Tape the fabric on top, so you can see the script through it. Using gold fabric paint and a fine paintbrush, trace the lettering onto the voile. Press the fabric, following the manufacturer's instructions, to set the color.*

three *To decorate wrapping paper, trace different types of writing onto tissue paper, using gold acrylic paint. Complement the wrapping paper with a bow of white or gold-trimmed organza ribbon.*

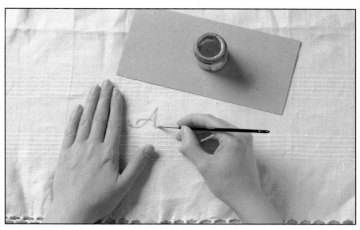

four *For the monogrammed hand towel, use paper cutouts to plan your design. Tape the chosen letter flat onto a work surface. Lay the towel over the alphabet, and tape flat. Trace over the letter onto the towel with the fabric paint.*

five *If you wish to apply an initial to a chair or other piece of furniture, put carbon paper onto the back of the photocopied lettering or rub all over the back with a soft pencil. Then transfer this to the furniture by going over the outline with a harder pencil. Paint over the outline and let dry.*

INDIAN SUMMER

THIS WINDOW SEAT RECESS was given a touch of glamorous Eastern mystery by layering fine, silky sari lengths behind each other to build up to a gloriously rich color. The sunlight picks up the gold embroidered flecks and braids, and the star lantern between the curtains casts its own magic spell. If you have never been in a sari shop, you will be amazed by the vast range of exquisitely patterned silks and voiles you can buy.

YOU WILL NEED

7 red and yellow sari lengths
(or fewer)
braid, 7 yards plus width of
each sari for
braid edging
iron-on hem tape
iron
needle
matching sewing thread
wooden curtain rod
drill
plastic anchors and hooks
wrought-iron curtain rod

one *If the saris do not have braid edges, add them with iron-on hem tape. Cut the remaining braid into 5½-inch lengths to make seven loops for each sari. Space them at equal distances along the tops, and slip-stitch. Put the wooden curtain rod through all the loops of three saris and fix it into the recess with hooks. Hang the iron rod on the outer frame, and hang two saris on the left by threading their loops alternately so that one hangs in front. Hang the two other saris on the right.*

two *Separate the red and yellow saris, holding one in each hand about halfway down their length.*

three *Wrap the yellow one around the red one and knot them together. Arrange the folds of the knot so that the fabric tumbles away and spills to the floor.*

INDIAN TEMPLE BED

INDIAN TEMPLE WALL PAINTINGS are the inspiration for this arch-shaped headboard. The bedroom feels as if it has been magically transported thousands of miles, but the real magic here comes in a simple can of paint. Before painting the headboard, set the mood with a deep rust-colored wash on the walls. If you can, use a water-based limewash for an authentic powdery bloom. If you are using latex, thin it with water.

YOU WILL NEED

large roll of brown packing paper

felt-tipped pen

masking tape (optional)

scissors

spray adhesive

chalk

water-based paint: dark blue, bright blue and red

plate

kitchen sponge

sandy cream latex paint

medium and fine paintbrushes

fine-grade sandpaper

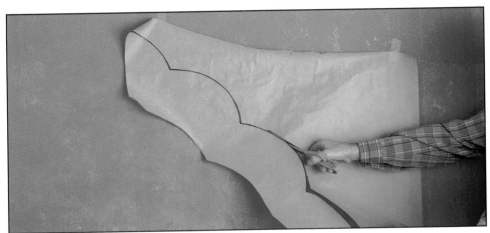

one *Refer to the diagram on the right that shows the shape of the arch. Transfer a half-arch onto brown packing paper, enlarging it as required using a grid system. Alternatively, tape a sheet of brown packing paper on the wall and draw the half-arch directly onto it, following the pattern shape. Cut out using a pair of scissors.*

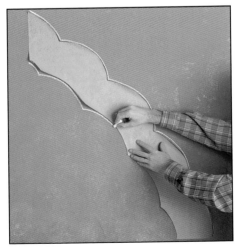

two *Position the paper pattern on the wall with spray adhesive and draw around the edges with chalk.*

three *Flip the pattern and draw around it to produce the second half of the arch. Spread some dark blue paint onto a plate and use a damp sponge to dab it onto the central panel. Don't cover the background completely, but let some of the wall color show through. When the paint is dry, apply the bright blue paint over the dark blue in the same way.*

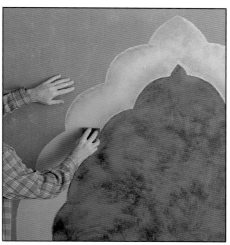

four *When the paint is dry, paint the arch in sandy cream latex, using a medium-sized paintbrush. When the latex paint is dry, rub it back in places with fine-grade sandpaper to give a faded effect. Outline the inside and outside of the arch with the red paint, using a fine paintbrush. Support your painting hand with your free hand and use the width of the brush to make a single line. Outline the outer red stripe with a thinner dark blue line.*

five *Let dry, then use fine-grade sandpaper to soften any hard edges and give the arch the naturally faded appearance of an old temple wall.*

FOUR-POSTER SARI

THE DRAPES FOR THIS four-poster bed have been made from lengths of beautifully colored traditional sari fabric and ribbons. Whether wrapped, folded or tucked, they do not appear at all bulky. Most saris have border designs and end pieces, with quite plain central areas. The saris used here are made from organza, and the yellow and orange panels have been hung alternately around three sides of the bed.

YOU WILL NEED

8 sari lengths

pins

needle

matching sewing threads

16½ yards ribbon or braid

scissors

tape measure

self-adhesive Velcro dots (optional)

cushion pad

1 yard silk fabric

square cushion tassels (optional)

one *Pin and sew a length of ribbon or braid along the top of each sari to reinforce the fabric. Cut six 12-inch lengths of ribbon or braid per sari for loops. Pin the ribbon lengths along the top of each sari, about 11½ inches apart. Turn under one end of each ribbon and slip-stitch to the sari, leaving the other end loose.*

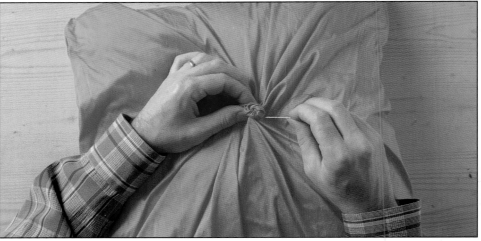

two *Hang the saris from the four-poster. Loop the ribbons around the rail. Sew the loose ends with a few small slip-stitches, or use self-adhesive Velcro dots.*

three *Place the cushion pad in the center of the fabric. Loosely fold two sides of the fabric over it, then fold the other two sides over them. Slip-stitch the back seam, but do not pull the fabric tightly around the cushion pad. Turn the cushion over. Pull up the fabric in the center and twist into a decorative knot. Hold the knot in place with a few stitches. Decorate with tassels in a shade of the same color, if desired.*

PISTACHIO-SHELL BORDER

IN INDIA, THE DECORATION on floors and walls is as varied as the materials available. The floors of temples and shrines are often intricately patterned with natural objects, such as seeds, shells and stones. Restrict your decoration to places where you don't normally wear shoes. You can fill in just a small area or a whole border. A corner about 4 x 4 feet takes about 7 pounds of unshelled pistachio nuts.

YOU WILL NEED

cream latex paint

paint roller

paint-mixing tray

ruler

pencil

masking tape

blue acrylic eggshell paint

paintbrushes

white glue

pistachio shells

natural sponge

eggshell latex paint: peach, cream and pale blue

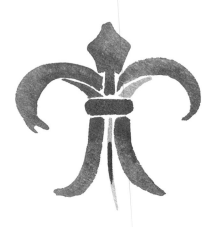

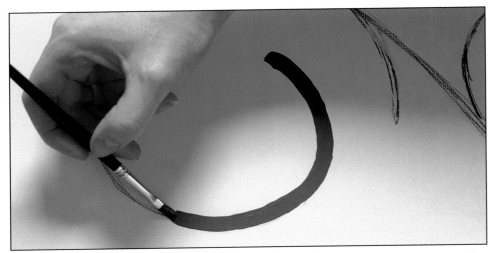

one *Make sure your floor surface is sound, dry and level; cover with hardboard or marine-plywood if necessary. Apply a base coat of cream latex. Measure and draw out your straight borders and edge them with masking tape. Draw your curved shapes straight on to the floor free-hand or using a traced shape. Fill in the lines with blue paint.*

two *Apply plenty of thick white glue to a small blue area. Apply the shells, working on the fine areas first. You may find you need to grade the shells by size, in advance.*

three *When the glue is dry, paint blue over the shells and touch up any cream areas that need it. Randomly sponge the area inside the border, with the darkest color first.*

four *Let dry completely and then repeat, using a softer shade of the same color (in the photograph, peach mixed with cream). Let dry and then use the same technique to apply a new color (in the photograph, pale blue) over it.*

five *Seal the floor with watered-down glue, as recommended by the manufacturer; it should be applied thickly over the shells. The whiteness will disappear as it dries, leaving a clear surface. Let dry completely.*

FILIGREE WOODEN PANEL

RADIATOR PANELING NEED not be used only for its original purpose; it can also be used to create an unusual wall covering. It often comes in a variety of interesting designs that make it worth using over a much larger area. Turn it on its side and attach it above a skirting board to bring it up to chair-rail height. When choosing the colors, bear in mind that the background must be strong enough to show through the paneling.

YOU WILL NEED

scrap paper

pencil

ruler

radiator paneling

white china pencil

jigsaw or hacksaw

latex paint in 2 colors

paintbrushes

paint roller

paint-mixing tray

level

straightedge

drill, with masonry and wood bits

plastic anchors

hammer

wood screws

glue gun and glue sticks

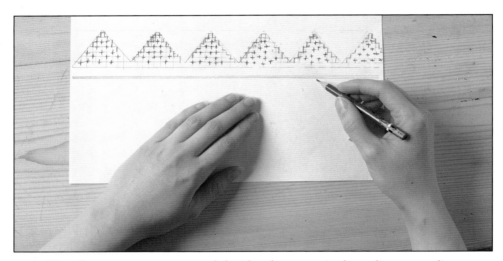

one *Plan the pattern on paper and decide where cuts in the radiator paneling are necessary. Mark off the sections to be cut out with a china pencil. Use a jig-saw or hacksaw to remove them. Choose the color.*

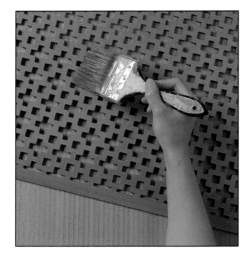

two *Paint the wall and let dry. Meanwhile, paint the paneling. Using a level and straightedge, mark a horizontal guideline for attaching the paneling to the wall.*

three *Drill holes in the wall for the paneling. Hammer plastic anchors into the holes. Drill holes in the paneling to correspond with the plastic anchors. Screw the paneling in position on the wall. Glue the paneling to the wall here and there, with the glue gun, to hold it flat against the wall. Then attach the border above. You can place a chair-rail between the two, if desired.*

TEXTURED GOLD FLOOR

EXOTIC SOUVENIRS FROM far-flung places sometimes require a dramatic backdrop to set them off. Gold and copper are suitably flamboyant, but texture is also needed. Builders' scrim, used to reinforce plaster, fits the bill. It gives a surface that traps different amounts of gold and copper, creating the effect of beaten metal. As with all exotic finishes, the delight is more in the instant transformation than in practicality.

YOU WILL NEED
tape measure
pencil
paper
ruler
power sander, with fine-grade sandpaper
builders' scrim
scissors
white glue
oil-based gold paint
wide paintbrush
copper powder paint
heavy-duty floor varnish

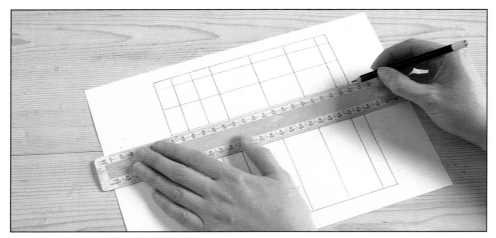

one *Measure the floor. Take into account the width of the scrim, plan your design on paper first to make sure that your pattern doesn't leave awkward half lines at the edges. You may need to lay marine-plywood or hardboard to ensure a smooth, flat surface. Lightly sand the floor to make sure it's perfectly flat.*

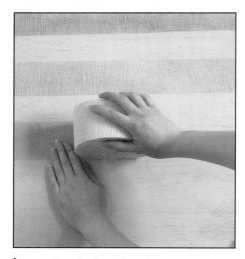

two *Cut the lengths of scrim, starting with the longest, and lay it to your pattern. Conceal seams where two lengths cross underneath, overlapping the ends by at least 6 inches.*

three *Stick the scrim down with white glue. Brush out any glue that soaks through to the top to hold the scrim firmly. Don't worry if you spread glue outside the area of the scrim. Pencil in a few guidelines and put a weight on the other end of the scrim to keep it straight. Dilute the glue with water and coat the whole floor.*

four *Paint on the gold paint, covering the whole floor. If using an oil-based paint, ensure that you have plenty of ventilation in the room.*

five *When the paint is dry, dust the copper powder paint over the scrim, letting it be trapped by the mesh surface. Apply at least two coats of heavy-duty floor varnish to seal.*

AMERICAN DREAM

LIE IN STATE EVERY NIGHT, draped in the stars and stripes or any brightly colored flag that takes your fancy. This is a great bed-covering idea, and different rooms can have different flags to complement different color schemes. The timber-clad walls and peg-rail above the bed give the room a ranch-house feel that looks great alongside brilliant red, white and blue.

YOU WILL NEED

2 large flags
pillow
package of safety pins
wooden buttons
needle and thread
quilt

one *Fold one of the flags around the pillow and use safety pins to close the long seam.*

two *Sew three wooden buttons along one pillow edge to hold the seam closed. Leave the other edge open so the pillow can be removed.*

three *Select an assortment of wooden buttons to attach around the edge and across the center of the second flag.*

four *Lay the flag over the quilt. Sew on the buttons, stitching through both the flag and the quilt, so that the layers are held together.*

SHELL-SHOCKED

AFTER A VACATION, MAKE your shell collection into something really special. We have used them to decorate fine voile curtains, and added interest with eyelets along the top threaded with string loops. Also following this theme, an easy, effective way of trimming a wall is with a length of fine rope attached at chair-rail height. Attach a row of tiny shells above. To complete the look, paint a terra-cotta pot white and attach a small sanddollar to the front.

YOU WILL NEED

iron-on interfacing (optional)

tape measure

dressmaker's scissors

cotton voile, the required drop, plus 4 x the window width

dressmaker's pins

needle and basting thread

sewing machine

matching sewing thread

chrome eyelets

hammer

wooden block

rough natural string

fine beading wire

glue gun and glue sticks

electric drill, with very fine drill bit (optional)

beading needle (optional)

terra-cotta pot

matte white latex paint

paintbrush

sanddollar

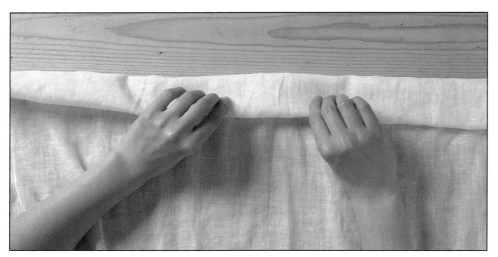

one *To give extra body to the headings of fine fabrics, cut a length of iron-on interfacing 2 inches wide and bond it to the wrong side of the voile. Pin, baste, press and machine-stitch the heading across the top and the hem at the bottom. Then turn under a ½-inch hem down each side. Pin, baste, press and sew. Mark the positions of the eyelets with pins.*

two *Attach the eyelets, following the manufacturer's instructions. Find a secure surface when hammering the eyelets in place.*

three *Cut equal lengths of string, thread the strings through the eyelets and knot the ends. Cut lengths of wire and use a glue gun to stick them onto the shells. Alternatively, drill holes in the shells. A combination of these methods may be helpful, depending on the shape of the shells. Position the shells on the curtains.*

four *Use the beading wire to "sew" the shells on to the curtain by hand, as invisibly as possible.*

five *Paint the terra-cotta pot white. Put a little glue on the side of the pot and attach the sanddollar.*

SHEER MAGIC

TRIM A PLAIN LINEN or burlap bed cover and pillowcase with the sheerest of voile fabrics to create a look that is simple, tailored and elegant. Large bone buttons and the rougher textures of burlap and linen are the perfect foil to the fineness of the fabric. Cut the voile slightly longer than the drop on the bed so it falls onto the floor all around. The amount of voile given here is for a double bed, but the idea can be adapted to suit any bed size.

YOU WILL NEED

tape measure
about 7½ yards cotton voile
dressmaker's scissors
dressmaker's pins
needle
basting thread
sewing machine
matching sewing thread
16 large bone buttons
fine embroidery scissors
tapestry needle
fine string
burlap or fine linen bed cover
pillow

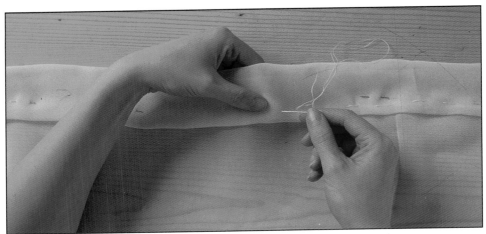

one *For the top of the cover, you will need a piece of voile the length of the bed plus the drop on one end. The piece should be 6 inches narrower than the width of the bed so the buttons will not be too near the edge. Allow 4 inches all around for double hems. For the sides, you will need two pieces the length of the bed. Measure the drop from the buttons to the floor, allowing 4 inches for hems as before. Pin, baste and sew all the hems.*

two *Mark the position of the buttons and button-holes. They must correspond exactly. Sew the button-holes, then cut the centers carefully. Use a tapestry needle and fine string to sew the buttons in position on the burlap bed cover, and button the voile cover on top.*

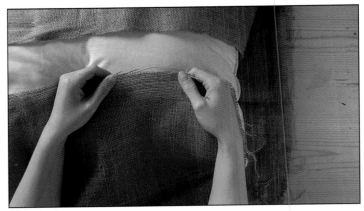

three *For the pillowcase, cut a piece of burlap the depth of the pillow and twice the length, plus seam allowances on the long sides. With right sides together, pin, baste and sew the top and bottom edges. Turn right side out and press.*

four *To make a fringed edge, find a thread running across the pillow, just in from the cut edge. Pull gently to fray the edge. Use the same method to make an over-cover for the pillow from voile. Hem all the edges.*

five *Mark the position of the button-holes in each corner. Machine-stitch the button-holes and cut the centers. Sew buttons onto the corners of the burlap pillow cover, and button the voile cover over the top.*

CALICO TENT

GET THAT VACATION FEELING every morning when you look out on the day from your tent. This could make a novelty bedhead for a child's bedroom or a stylish feature in a adult's bedroom. The tent is made using a combination of attachments intended for different purposes. The chrome rods are shower rails, finished off in copper with plumber's pipe caps. The thin copper tube is also from the plumbing department—it has an attractive finish and can be bent easily with long-nosed pliers. The stability of the tent is assured by the use of shower rail sockets on the wall and a line of cup hooks on the ceiling. The fabric used here is unbleached calico.

YOU WILL NEED

8¾ x 1 yards unbleached calico

tape measure

pencil and ruler

scissors

6½ yards iron-on hemming tape

iron

hacksaw

60-inch length chrome shower rail

center punch

hammer

drill, with bit (the size of the copper tube)

1 yard narrow copper tube

long-nosed pliers

3 chrome shower rail sockets

level

screwdriver

6 chrome cup hooks and plastic anchors

4½ yards white cord

3 copper pipe caps (to fit shower rail)

one *Decide on the height of the top of the tent. Measure the fabric and tear it to size. Fold the fabric in four to find the center and mark this point. Measure 14 inches down each short edge and mark the points.*

two *Draw a connecting line between the center point and each of the side points to give the shape for the top.*

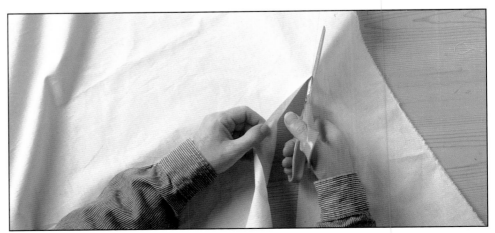

three *Cut along the drawn lines, then cut a 1¼-inch notch at each of the points of the tent shape. Fold the fabric over to make a 1¼-inch seam around the top and sides of the fabric.*

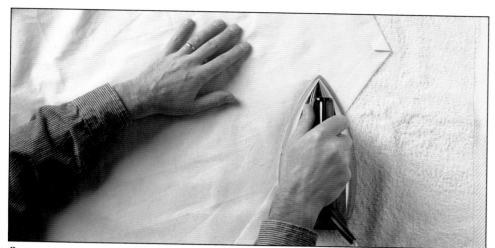

four *Use iron-on hemming tape to hold down the seams neatly. The two pieces should now meet at a right angle to make the tent shape. The sides and top of the tent will fold back to give a double thickness of fabric. Make three holes for the rails at the corner points and reinforce the fabric with an extra square of calico ironed on with hemming tape.*

five *Use a hacksaw to cut the length of chrome shower rail into three 20-inch pieces.*

six *Use a center punch to dent the shower rail where the holes will be drilled, so that the drill does not slip. You will need to drill a hole 2 inches from one end of two of the poles and two holes in the other pole, the first 2 inches from one end and the second ½ inch in from it.*

seven *Drill the holes using a drill bit the same size as the copper tube. Use a hacksaw to cut two lengths of copper tube. Use the long-nosed pliers to bend one end of each copper tube into a hook shape. Use the chrome rail to estimate the curve of the hooks. Each hook should fit snugly around the chrome rail with its end fitting into the drilled hole.*

eight *Position the shower rail sockets on the wall so that the rails slot into them. Use a level to check that the outer two are level.*

CONTINUED OVER ➤

Above: The hooked copper tubes fit over and into the chrome rail. The cord is looped around the rail and crossed over to suspend the tent front from the cup hooks. The side rails are finished off with the copper caps and suspended from a crossed cord attached to the cup hooks.

nine *Refer to the diagram below. Push the chrome rails through the holes in the back of the tent, then put the copper tubes in place to hold the front section rigid. Put the straight end of each copper tube into the hole in each side rail. Put the hooked ends over the middle rail and into the two drilled holes. Attach a row of cup hooks to the ceiling directly above the front edge of the tent. Loop white cord around the cup hooks and the chrome rails for added stability. Finally, cap the chrome pipes with the copper caps.*

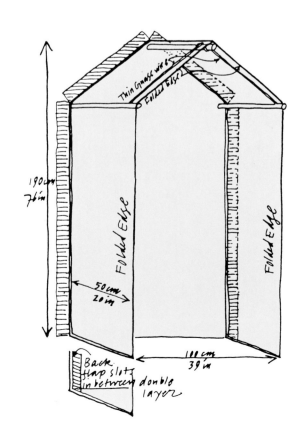

SEASIDE SETTING

SOOTHE THE SOUL AND mind by strolling along the beach and, at the same time, searching the shoreline for all kinds of wonderful things: strands of seaweed, pieces of driftwood, soft gray pebbles, birds' feathers, pearly seashells and chalky white stones with holes ready-made for threading onto pieces of twine. Make the most of your natural treasures by using them to decorate mirrors, picture frames and trinket boxes, or any other unadorned objects—their uses are endless. Seashells also make wonderfully evocative candle holders.

YOU WILL NEED

DRIFTWOOD AND PEBBLE FRAMES

distressed-wood frames

white glue (optional)

medium-grade sandpaper

wood stain and paintbrush (optional)

about 20 inches thick rope

staple gun or hammer and nails

driftwood

glue gun and glue sticks

seaweed

pebbles and stones

seashells

PEBBLE AND GLASS NECKLACES

raffia

tiny pebbles

smooth colored glass

glue gun and glue sticks

SHELL CANDLEHOLDERS

burnt-down candles

kitchen knife

seashells

safety matches

one *For the driftwood frame, reglue the seams, if necessary. Sand it along the grain and stain it, if desired. To hang the mirror, attach the rope to the top of the frame, with a staple gun or hammer and nails. Arrange the driftwood pieces around the frame. Experiment with different positions until you are happy with the result.*

two *Use a glue gun to attach the driftwood in place, making sure the pieces are perfectly secure.*

three *Work out the position of the seaweed so it drapes gently across the mirror. Add the pebbles, stones and shells, raising them slightly off the edge so they are reflected in the mirror. Glue the pebbles and other materials in place.*

four *For the pebble frame, use a similar frame base to the driftwood frame and sand and stain as before, if required. Select a pleasing variety of stones. Arrange them to your liking and glue them on the frame.*

five *For the pebble and glass necklace, tie a length of raffia around tiny pebbles and pieces of smooth colored glass. Use a glue gun to apply a tiny dot of glue to each knot where the pebble or glass is tied. For the candles in shells, cut the candles right down with a knife and stand them in a shell. Light the candles and let the wax drip down until it fills the shells. Blow out the flame. The wax then solidifies to the shape of the shell.*

BUTTERFLY MONTAGE

SURREALISM AND THE WORK of artists such as Ernst, Escher, and Magritte inspire surprising ways of depicting unusual yet familiar objects in designs for montages. This butterfly floor could easily have been made using motifs of flowers, boats or chairs. Strong lines are important, and there are books of wonderful line drawings available. Lay the motifs down in an ordered pattern. Here, the design suggests the flight of butterflies. Protect the montage from wear and tear by applying half a dozen coats of varnish.

YOU WILL NEED

light-colored latex paint

paintbrushes

motifs

craft knife

self-healing cutting mat

wallpaper paste and brush

indelible felt-tipped pen or fine artist's brush and oil-based paints

matte varnish

one *Make sure your floor is completely smooth. If necessary, lay a hardboard or marine-plywood floor. Paint the floor a light color so that the motifs will show up. Photocopy your chosen image(s) in at least seven sizes, ranging from quite small to fairly large.*

two *Using a craft knife and a cutting mat, carefully cut out every image.*

three *Decide on the positions of your images and stick them in place with wallpaper paste.*

four *Add remaining fine details with an indelible felt-tipped pen or a fine artist's brush. Finish by applying at least six coats of varnish to be sure of its durability (some acrylic varnishes dry very quickly) or apply a very strong floor varnish.*

BILLOWING MUSLIN

FLOATY BUTTER-COLORED MUSLIN IS one of the cheapest ways to cover a large window without blocking out all the light. The muslin here is in two pieces, each long enough to drape over the rail and down to the floor on both sides. One of the lengths was stamped with a sponge cutout in the shape of a melon half. The two pieces were hung next to each other and knotted about halfway down so the stamped half crosses over to the other side.

YOU WILL NEED

tracing paper

pencil

thin cardboard, for template

block of high-density foam
(the type used for camping
mattresses)

craft knife

2 lengths butter-colored
muslin

2 bamboo poles, window
width

sewing machine (optional)

needle

matching sewing thread

fabric paint: coffee-brown
and dark brown

plate

paint roller or brush

tape

drill, and masonry bit

plastic anchors and cup
hooks

bundle of natural-colored
raffia

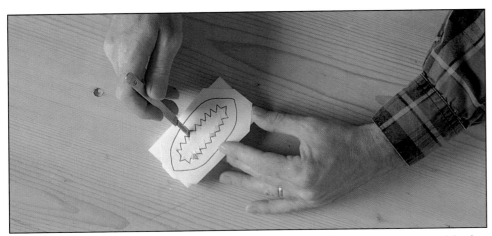

one *Trace the template, enlarging to the required size. Place it on the foam block, then cut around it. Scoop out the inner area, leaving the printing surface intact. Fold both of the muslin lengths in half. Form a channel along the top of each, about 2 inches down from the fold. It must be the width of the two bamboo poles, as they will slide into it. Sew by machine or hand.*

two *Put some of the coffee-brown fabric paint onto the plate and run the roller through it until it is thoroughly and evenly coated. Use the roller to ink the foam stamp.*

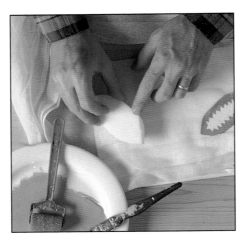

three *Start stamping the pattern, rotating the stamp in your hand each time you print. Leave more or less the same amount of space between prints.*

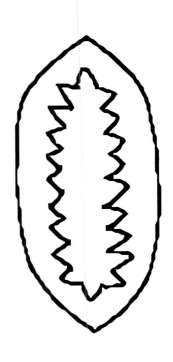

four *Stamp darker prints randomly among lighter ones. Set the fabric paint according to the manufacturer's instructions. Tape over the ends of the bamboo poles so that they do not catch on the muslin, and slide them through the sewn channels in the curtains.*

five *Drill holes and insert the plastic anchors and cup hooks in the top of the window recess, about 4–6 inches in from the sides. Cut ten 18-inch strips of raffia and use five on either side, twisted together into a rope, to bind the bamboo poles together in place of the tape. Use the loose ends to suspend the bamboo rail by tying them to the cup hooks. Tie a knot with the two curtains about halfway down their length. Experiment with different effects, but take your time over the positioning of the knot, its shape and the way the muslin drapes over it.*

CORRUGATED HEADBOARD

CORRUGATED CARDBOARD HAS been liberated from its role as a packaging material, as designers realize its potential and versatility. It is strong, rigid, insulating, economical and light as a feather. This project celebrates the natural cardboard color, but colored sheets are also available and are great for adding decorative touches. Corrugated cardboard is perfect for experimentation, especially as it is so inexpensive.

YOU WILL NEED

glue gun and glue sticks

2 x 1 inch lengths wood to fit around the edges of the medium-density fiberboard

rectangle of medium-density fiberboard, to fit behind the bed

roll of corrugated cardboard 1 yard high

triangle

scissors

staple gun and staples

ruler

pencil

scalpel or craft knife

cutting mat or cardboard

small rubber roller

one *Use the glue gun to stick the thin lengths of wood to the back of the fiberboard around the edges. This will be hidden, so any glue drips will not show. Place a large piece of corrugated cardboard over the front of the fiberboard. Use a triangle to press against and crease the cardboard neatly for folding at the corners. Fold the cardboard neatly around the corners in the same way that you would wrap a package.*

two *Trim away any excess cardboard that may cause the corners to look bulky. Staple the flaps down, pressing the gun firmly against the cardboard from above to prevent any kickback that may cause the staples to protrude.*

three *Carefully staple the cardboard along the strips of wood, keeping it taut as you go along. Cut four strips of cardboard 3 inches wide, and approximately 18 inches long. Use the rubber roller to flatten down the ridges. Fold the strips into thirds along their length, so that they are 1 inch wide. Again, use the rubber roller to flatten the strips.*

four *Position the strips to form a diamond shape in the center of the headboard. Allow the ends to overlap each other. Staple the strips in place. Cut through the two overlapping layers with scissors to miter the corners. Staple the strips as closely as possible to the mitered ends.*

five *For the spiral turrets, cut seven 20-inch strips of cardboard. One long edge of each strip is cut at an angle: Cut the first two strips along a line sloping from one short edge of 4 inches to the other short edge of 2 inches. Cut the second two strips from one edge of 4¾ inches to the other of 2 inches. Cut the next two from 5½ inches to 2 inches. Cut the last strip from 6¼ inches to 2 inches. Starting at the wider end, roll up the cardboard with the ridges on the outside. Keep the base straight. Use the glue gun to stick down the end of each turret. Arrange the turrets on top of the headboard so that the tallest one is in the middle. Stick them down using the hot-glue gun. Use plenty of glue in the middle and less toward the outside to achieve a good bond without any mess.*

THE NEW WAVE

CORRUGATED CARDBOARD IS A much-maligned material that can look absolutely stunning if used innovatively. It is easy to work with and has myriad uses. Experiment with different shapes to see which looks most pleasing. Triangles would look great bordering a door frame, for example, and perhaps following the lines of the skirting. Bear in mind that corrugated paper crushes very easily, so before starting work, flatten it with a ruler.

YOU WILL NEED

tape measure

roll of natural corrugated cardboard

scissors

ruler

thin cardboard

pencil

craft knife

self-healing cutting mat

spray adhesive

masking tape (optional)

candles

white latex paint

paintbrush

glue gun and glue sticks

natural string

straight-sided vase

fine corrugated paper in different colors

paper glue

one *Measure the width of the sill and cut the corrugated cardboard to this measurement, plus the required drop. Flatten the ridges with a ruler. Draw the design onto cardboard and cut out a template. Draw the shape on the natural corrugated paper, using the template. Cut it out with a craft knife on a cutting mat.*

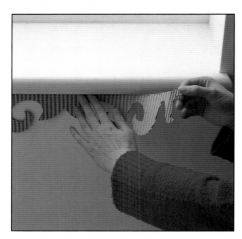

two *Spray the back of the corrugated cardboard with adhesive and attach in place. If you want to remove the decoration later, stick masking tape under the sill and glue the decoration to the tape.*

three *For the candle-wrappers, cut strips of corrugated paper to the right size and paint them with white latex. Slit the corrugations with scissors. Cut a wider strip and glue it to the back of the white strip. Wrap the decoration around the candles. Cut string long enough to wrap several times around the candles. Use the same technique to make a decoration for a straight-sided vase.*

four *To make the picture frame, measure the image that will be framed and decide on the size and shape required. Draw the frame backing onto corrugated cardboard and cut it out with the craft knife and ruler. Use the backing as a template to draw and cut out the front of the frame from colored corrugated paper. Cut out the central frame area. Stick the image in position with paper glue so the backing color shows through in a thin border all around.*

five *Make a stand for the frame, with a piece of corrugated cardboard cut to the shape shown. Decorate the frame with twisted strips of colored paper.*

CORRUGATED LAMP BASE

CORRUGATED CARDBOARD HAS SCULPTURAL qualities that elevate it from a boring packaging material. Its construction, with one smooth and one rigid side, means that it can be rolled into even, tubular shapes to make a lamp base. This is one project in which the fact that corrugated cardboard is very lightweight might be a disadvantage, so take care to site the lamp where it is unlikely to be knocked over.

YOU WILL NEED
roll of corrugated cardboard

ruler

pencil

scalpel and cutting mat

glue gun with all-purpose glue sticks

bottle adapter lamp fitting

one *Cut a 20¹/₂ x 13³/₄-inch rectangle of corrugated cardboard and roll it lengthwise, leaving the center hollow for the lamp fitting. Glue the loose edge.*

two *Cut a 53 x 1¹/₂-inch rectangle from the corrugated cardboard. Measure in 7¹/₄ inches from the top-left corner, draw a line between this point and the bottom-right corner and cut along this line. Apply glue to the square end and line it up with the column base. Wrap it around, gluing to hold the layers together. Keep the base flat.*

three *Cut a 20¹/₂ x 1¹/₂-inch rectangle of corrugated cardboard, then glue and wrap it around the base to add extra stability.*

four *Cut another 53 x 1¹/₂-inch rectangle of corrugated cardboard, then glue and wrap this around the top of the column. Keep the top flat. Ask an electrician to install the bottle adapter lamp fitting and to wire it to a cord.*

Novelty Rooms

THIS IS THE PERFECT place to let your imagination run riot, with customized designs for adults and children. But a word of warning—if you plan to decorate a child's room, first ask the occupant. You may think Pooh Bear makes an excellent wall stencil, but younger decorators may be thinking along the lines of not-so-cuddly extinct creatures...

Whatever you decide on should be regarded as temporary. The first rule of decorating a child's bedroom is not to do anything that can't be changed easily. Tastes change and fads go as quickly as they arrive. Bearing this in mind, make everything as big, bright and bold as possible. You may not agree with the aesthetics of it all, but a room with a sense of humor is a lot of fun—and a stimulating environment for children, especially if they feel able to let themselves go in it. That means don't be too dainty about the room. Everything should be as practical and durable as possible.

Such a decorating challenge opens up endless opportunities. For the floor, choose different colored carpet tiles arranged as for a board game. Kids like writing on walls, so let them—provide a wall-to-wall blackboard with a colorful border.

Comic strips are recognized everywhere, and a montage of well-known characters can be used for a striking decorative focal point in a teenager's bedroom.

Laundry baskets topped with brightly colored domes make great storage containers. Stencil the walls with flags, which are colorful and easy to prepare, or simply turn a wall into a patchwork of color. Our secret for getting the perfect finish is so easy the kids can do it.

Budding astronauts will love the padded headboard covered with space blankets, and you can make individual duvet covers for each child.

Many of our ideas for stenciling and painting can be done by the children, so don't be shy about coming forward to ask for their help. And make sure they have their say about what they want. Their coolness quotient may depend on it.

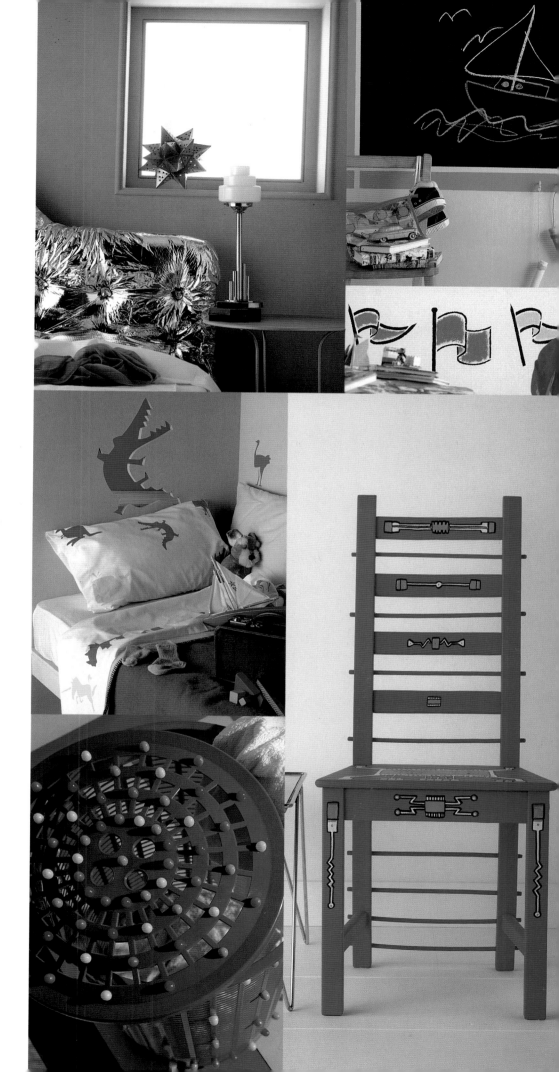

WALL BLACKBOARD

THIS SIMPLE BLACKBOARD is lots of fun and a highly practical wall treatment for a child's bedroom or playroom. Make sure the wall is flat before you start, and paint it with undercoat and two coats of latex first, if necessary. Bear the height of the child in mind when you are deciding on the size and position of the blackboard. Blackboard paint is available at most good paint suppliers.

YOU WILL NEED

tape measure
pencil
level
straightedge
masking tape
blackboard paint
paintbrushes
latex paint in several colors
tracing paper (optional)
craft knife (optional)
self-healing cutting mat
(optional)
stencil brush
hooks
string
chunky chalks

one *Measure and draw the blackboard and the border on the wall, using the level and straightedge. Mask off the blackboard with tape and apply two coats of blackboard paint. Remove the masking tape immediately. Let dry.*

two *Mask off the border and paint with two coats of latex. Remove the masking tape immediately.*

three *Mask off the diamond shape or draw and cut a stencil from tracing paper, using the craft knife and cutting mat. Tape it to the wall. Paint the diamonds with a stencil brush. Paint the hooks. Screw them into the wall and attach the chalks.*

FLAG STENCILS

HERE'S A STRONG DESIGN to add lively color and an element of fun to a child's room, while avoiding the conventional and rather predictable motifs and colors available on ready-made children's wallpapers. The easiest way to make a unique stencil is to photocopy a simple motif onto acetate: Here, two complementary flag motifs are combined. Use the stencils as a border at picture- or chair-rail height, randomly around the room or in straight lines to make a feature of, for example, a chimney on one wall or an alcove behind a desk or bookshelves.

YOU WILL NEED

sheet of acetate
craft knife
self-healing cutting mat
tape
black latex paint
stencil brush or small paintbrush
latex paint in several bright colors

one *Photocopy the designs from the back of the book in various sizes to try them out. When you are happy with the size, photocopy them directly onto the acetate.*

two *Cut out the stencils carefully, using a craft knife and cutting mat. Tape the stencil to the wall.*

three *Stencil a bold outline in black.*

four *Use a stencil brush to apply color inside the outline, or paint it free-hand for a looser, more appropriate effect for a child's room.*

PURPLE PLAYROOM

THESE LUSH PURPLE FELT drapes knock the socks off most playroom curtains. They are inspired by the felt shapes that children play with. There is a wide range of topics available —from farms to fairies. When you press out the pre-cut shapes you get a great negative shape as well as your motif. The curtains are attached to a narrow strip of wood, extending 8 inches beyond the frame on both sides above the window.

YOU WILL NEED

strip of wood 2 x 1 inch thick

level

drill, and masonry bit

plastic anchors and screws

screwdriver

pinking shears

deep purple felt, 2 yards wide x the drop plus 16 inches

commercial pre-cut felt shapes

fabric glue

chalk

thumb tacks

staple gun (optional)

one *Attach the strip of wood above the window extending at least 8 inches beyond the frame on both sides. Use pinking shears to cut two strips of curtain felt the width of the curtain fabric and ³/4 inch deeper than the pre-cut felt squares. Stick the felt backgrounds along the strips with fabric glue, allowing space for the gathers.*

two *Stick the strips on the wrong side of the top edge of the curtains (i.e. the side that will not be decorated). On the right side of the curtain, draw a chalk line 16 inches from the top. Pin the curtain edges to meet in the center of the strip of wood, holding the top 16 inches above it. Pin the outside edges to each end of the strip of wood.*

three *Pin or staple the curtains into pleats. If you use pins, you can adjust the pleats as you go. When the pleating is complete, let the valance flop down.*

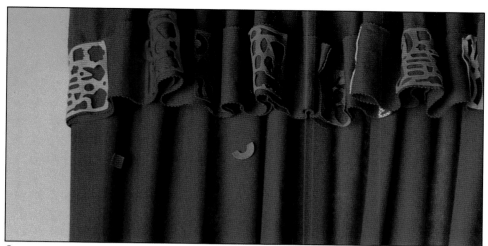

four *Arrange all the felt shapes randomly on the curtains. They will cling for long enough for you to make a design you like. Stick the shapes in place with fabric glue.*

five *You can make tiebacks in the same style as the valance.*

$\mathscr{B}$EADED LAUNDRY BASKET

BRIGHTLY COLORED PLASTIC laundry baskets are cheap and practical, but they need help to give them a more individual look. This purple laundry basket was made glamorous with bright Chinese checker pieces taken from an inexpensive children's set. They are ideal, as the domed pieces have spiked backs that can be trimmed to the required depth and glued into holes drilled in the plastic. The attachments are secure, so don't worry about beads scattering all over the bedroom floor. This decorated basket is not suitable for children under three, who might swallow the checker pieces and choke.

YOU WILL NEED
Chinese checker pieces
wire cutters
plastic laundry basket with lid
drill, with fine bit
glue gun with all-purpose
glue sticks (or all-purpose
glue)
masking tape

one *Sort the Chinese checker pieces into colors. Trim the spikes so that the pieces will fit into the depth of the plastic basket without protruding on the other side.*

two *Drill holes for the spikes—a circle on the lid and lines down the sides.*

three *Sort the pieces into the color sequence you want. Apply glue to one spike at a time and push it into a hole. The glue sets quickly, so work fast.*

four *Run a length of masking tape around the base of the basket as a positioning guide for a straight band of colored pieces. Attach these as you did the other pieces.*

CHILD'S BEDROOM NOOK

CHILDREN LIKE THE security of enclosed sleeping spaces, and older children relish the privacy, especially if the room is shared with a brother or sister. In this project, fiberboard panels are positioned around an existing bed. They can be attached to the bed base or simply rested in a corner so that they enclose the space but cannot be pushed over. The stencils used to decorate the fiberboard panels and the bed linen can also be used on the walls.

YOU WILL NEED

2 sheets medium-density fiberboard, 48 inches x width of the bed

1 sheet medium-density fiberboard, 48 inches x length of the bed, plus 2 inches

2 x 1 inch strip wood, 48 inches long

drill, with size 10 bit

screwdriver and suitable screw attachments

pale gray latex paint

paintbrush

paper

spray adhesive

stencil cardboard

scalpel or craft knife

cutting mat or thick cardboard

white pillowcase

iron

masking tape

fabric paint: red, blue, yellow

plate

stencil brushes

white sheet or duvet cover

soft and hard pencils

jigsaw

fine-grade sandpaper

stencil paints (optional)

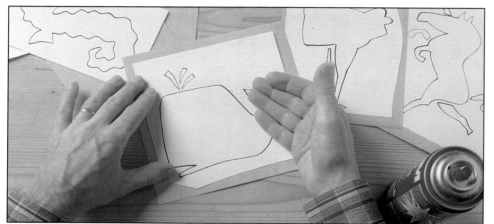

one *The shorter pieces of fiberboard are used for the head and foot of the bed. To make the bed surroundings, screw the strip of wood to butt up to one 48-inch edge of the head and foot pieces. Butt the long piece of fiberboard at right angles against the strip of wood on the bedhead and screw in place. Repeat with the foot, to make a three-sided surrounding for the bed. The bed surrounding will be stable, but it is advisable to put the long side against a wall. Paint the surrounding with gray latex.*

two *To stencil the bed linen, enlarge the templates overleaf onto paper. Spray the backs lightly with spray adhesive and stick them onto sheets of stencil cardboard. Cut out the stencils carefully, using a scalpel or craft knife on a cutting mat or sheet of thick cardboard to protect your work surface. Peel off the paper patterns.*

three *Wash and iron the pillowcase to be stenciled. Place some cardboard inside the pillowcase. Position the first stencil, holding it in place with masking tape.*

four *Spread each of the fabric paints onto the plate. Using a stencil brush, dab the first color onto the pillowcase. Apply the paint sparingly, as the color is best when built up gradually.*

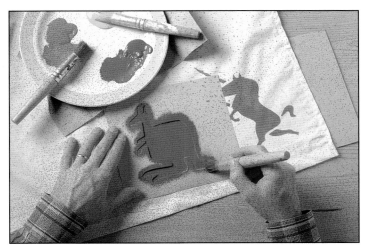

five *Position the next stencil, being very careful not to smudge the first one, and then stencil the second animal in another color.*

six *Position a third stencil and apply the final color. Continue alternating the stencils and colors to complete the pillowcase. Decorate the sheet or duvet cover in the same way.*

seven *To make the "window," enlarge the crocodile template in sections so that you end up with a good window-sized pattern. Then tape the different sections together. Rub the back of the pattern outline with a soft pencil.*

eight *Place the pattern faceup on the fiberboard and transfer by drawing over the outline with a hard pencil. Drill a hole at any point on the outline as the insertion point for the jigsaw blade.*

CONTINUED OVER ➤

nine *Use the jigsaw to cut out the crocodile shape. Work slowly and hold the blade vertically so that it cuts at its own speed without being pushed or dragged into the fiberboard. Rub down all the edges of the cut-out crocodile shape using fine-grade sandpaper.*

ten *Stencil a frieze of animals around the inside of the bed screen to coordinate with the bed linen. You can use the fabric paints for this, or matching stencil paints.*

ROBOT CHAIR

A SIMPLE CHAIR MAY not suit a dramatic paint treatment, but you can add to basic chairs to create more height or add drama with a ladder-back effect. The easiest addition to use is already turned dowel, available at lumberyards and do-it-yourself stores, which should be the thickness of your drill bit. If you are prepared for extra work in drilling out larger holes, all kinds of struts could be used, including twisted and carved pieces of the types used for shelving or balustrades. Decorating the chair with computer-age motifs in fluorescent paint adds further impact.

YOU WILL NEED
ladder-back chair
pencil
drill, with wood drill bit
ruler or measuring tape
saw
wooden dowels
medium-grade sandpaper
hammer
royal blue latex paint
medium and fine
paintbrushes
acrylic paint: white,
fluorescent yellow, green
and pink
permanent black marker
clear matte varnish

one *Mark the positions of the holes for the dowels. Drill all the holes. Keep the drill straight, or the dowel won't pass through both holes. Measure the back of the chair. Cut the dowels slightly longer than the chair back and sand the ends.*

two *Pass the dowel through one upright of the chair and line it up with the hole on the second upright.*

three *With a hammer, lightly tap the dowel through the second hole. Leave an equal amount of dowel showing on either side. Paint the whole chair with a blue base coat. Long, slow, even strokes will produce an even finish.*

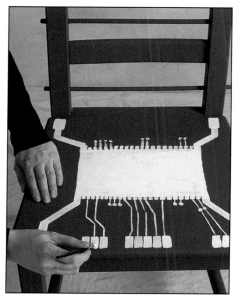

four *With a fine brush and white paint, sketch the outline for the "computer chip" design on the chair seat and on the wide struts of the back. The white provides a good base for the fluorescent paint. Again with a fine brush, paint on the design in yellow, green and pink fluorescent paints.*

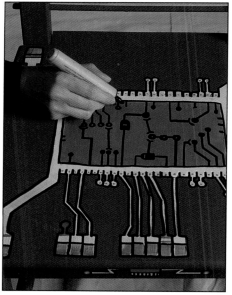

five *Outline the design with the marker and add any further detail. Finally, to protect all the paintwork, coat the whole chair with clear varnish.*

Space Bed

At last, a terrestrial bed with all the glamour and sparkle of space travel. If the very thought of bedtime has the kids reaching for sci-fi videos, why not let them relax wrapped in their very own shimmering silver "space-blanket" beds? The shape of this headboard is reminiscent of a 1950s tail fin, but you can choose almost any bold shape that can be cut out of fiberboard with a jigsaw. You can buy "space blankets" at outdoor-supply stores.

YOU WILL NEED

1 sheet medium-density fiberboard, width of the bed x height to bed base, plus approximately 1 yard

pen

ruler

string

thumb tack

jigsaw

fine-grade sandpaper

polyester duvet

staple gun and staples

thin silver insulating material

broad, woven adhesive tape

tape measure

thicker-textured silver insulating material (the type used under camping mattresses)

scissors

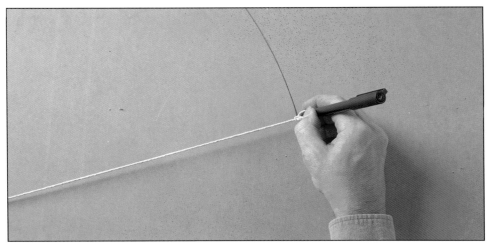

one *Draw a line across the width of the fiberboard about 16 inches down from the top edge. Tie a 16-inch length of string to a thumb tack and tie a pen to the other end. Push the pin into the line, just in from the left edge of the board. Pull the string taut and adjust its length to reach the top left-hand corner of the board. Using the string as the arm of a compass, draw a curve from the top of the board down to the horizontal line.*

two *Cut out the shape around the curve and along the line with a jigsaw. Sand down the edges.*

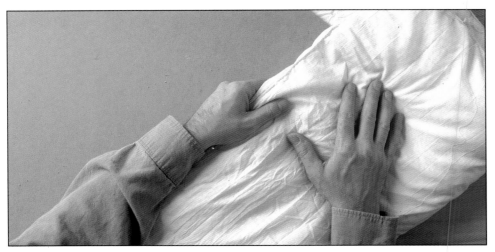

three *Fold the duvet around the fiberboard to create a smooth covering across the front. Fold the edges to the back.*

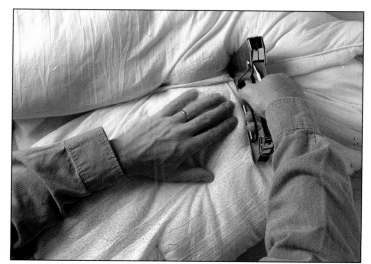

four *Staple the edges to the fiberboard, folding them under and tucking them in to get as even a finish as possible.*

five *Lay the covered shape onto the thin silver insulating material. Fold the edges to the back and staple.*

six *Stick a strip of broad woven adhesive tape over the edges of the silver material to cover the staples and give a neat finish.*

seven *Turn the bedhead over and adjust any wrinkles in the "space blanket."*

eight *Mark points at intervals of 9½ inches along a piece of string.*

nine *Use the piece of string to measure the positions of the quilting buttons on the covered headboard. Mark each point with a small square of woven tape.*

CONTINUED OVER ➤

ten *Cut strips of the thicker-textured insulating material into squares to use as "buttons" for the quilting.*

eleven *Staple a silver button on top of each tape square. Make sure that the silver covers up the tape. The tape strengthens the thin silver material and prevents the staples from tearing it.*

twelve *Push down hard with the staple gun, so that the staple penetrates right through to the fiberboard. Continue stapling the buttons in place until the whole headboard is quilted.*

COMIC-STRIP CHAIR

THIS MONTAGE IDEA HAS tons of impact and could be adapted to many different themes. Here, we have chosen comic-strip characters to create a chair that would be welcome in even the coolest teenager's bedroom. The seat cover could use any brightly colored logo or graphic cut from fabric, or make use of a favorite image by taking a picture to a store that transfers pictures onto T-shirts.

YOU WILL NEED

wooden-framed chair
medium-grade sandpaper
scissors
paper motifs
wallpaper paste
paintbrushes
clear gloss varnish or
spray gloss varnish
blue stretchy fabric
staple gun
fabric logo (optional)
fabric adhesive (optional)

one *Remove the seat from the chair. Sand the chair lightly all over to provide a key for the paste. Cut out the motifs carefully with sharp-pointed scissors. Apply paste carefully all over the back of the motifs. Let set until tacky.*

two *Brush wallpaper paste over the chair frame, then apply the motifs to the chair, using a brush to prevent tearing them while they are wet. Repeat until you have covered the whole chair. Let dry.*

three *Apply a coat of varnish to protect the chair. For the seat cushion, stretch the fabric over the cushion and staple it in place. Pull the fabric taut as you work around the cushion. If you wish to decorate the seat further, find a logo or graphic to go in the center. Apply fabric adhesive to the back and let it become tacky. Position and apply the logo to the seat cushion, pressing it down firmly until the glue has taken hold. Replace the cushion in the chair.*

BOARD GAME CARPET

ALONG WITH LINOLEUM TILES, carpet tiles are real winners in the practicality stakes. Almost unbeatable in areas that need to be hardwearing and where children and their accompanying wear and tear are concerned, carpet tiles have the single disadvantage that they never look like wall-to-wall carpet, no matter how well they are laid. Rather than fighting the fact that they come in non-fraying squares, make use of this very quality and create a fun floor-scape, such as this giant board game. Carpet tiles are very forgiving, allowing for slight discrepancies in cutting, and are very easy to replace if an area is damaged. A geometrical design is easiest; it is advisable to leave curves to the experts, but anything else, from a board game to the elegance of a painting by Mondrian, is accessible.

YOU WILL NEED

metal tape measure

pencil

paper

carpet tiles

white crayon or
white china pencil

metal ruler

rigid-bladed knife and plenty
of spare blades

heavy duty, double-sided
carpet tape

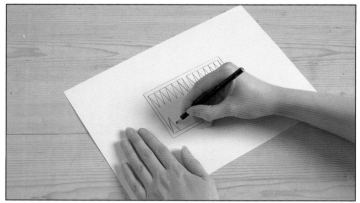

one *Measure your room and make sure that the floor is level and all protruding nails have been flattened. Any flat surface will accommodate the carpet tiles, whether it is marine-plywood, hardboard, floorboards or concrete. Plan your design on paper. Most rooms are not perfect rectangles, so leave room for an area of plain tiles to edge the pattern.*

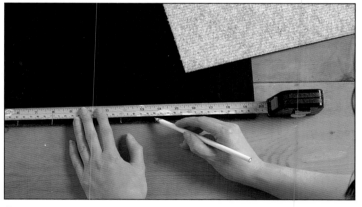

two *Measure the tiles to determine the size of your pointed shapes and to figure out how many tiles will be needed for your pattern. Consider the different weaves and nap of the carpet tiles, and make them work to enhance your chosen plan. Using a white crayon or china pencil, draw the pattern on the reverse of your tiles.*

◄

three *With a metal ruler and a rigid-bladed knife, score along the marked lines. Don't attempt to cut the tile through completely in one action. Starting at the top of the tile, cut down your scored lines. Do this on a solid surface and take extreme care while doing it.*

four *Lay down a line of carpet tape and remove the backing. Cut all the tiles for one complete run and place these first, rather than laying little bits at a time.*

five *Stick your cut tiles in place, making sure not to pack them too tightly. Begin by making the entire checkered border. Then fill in, laying strips of carpet tape as you work. Tread the tiles down; uneven cuts will be unnoticeable.*

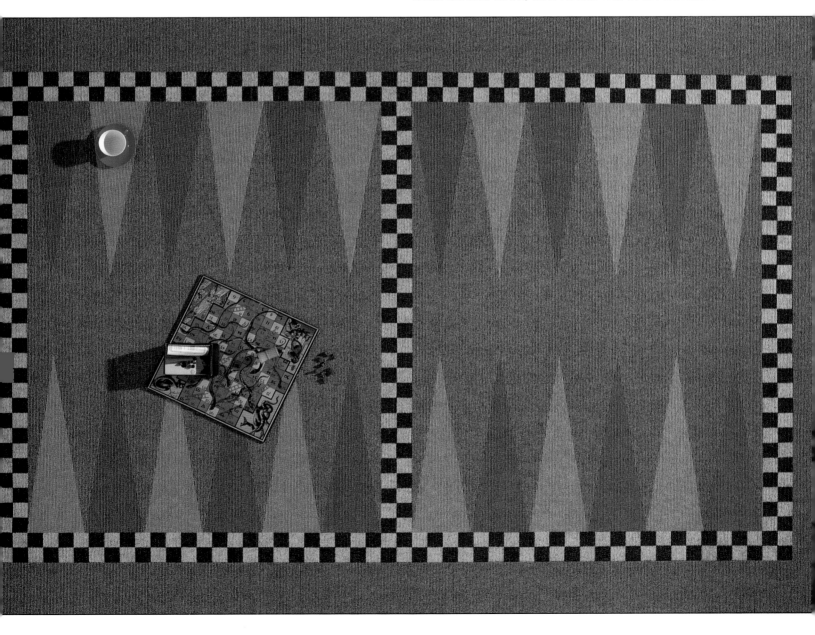

ℳINIBUS TOYBOX

EVERY CHILD SHOULD BE ENCOURAGED to put away his or her toys at the end of the day. This eye-catching toybox might just do the trick. The pastel-colored patches behind the bus stamps give the box a 1950s look. These are stenciled onto a light turquoise background. Stamp the buses on randomly so that some extend beyond the background shapes. Keep changing the angle of the stamp—the effect will be almost three-dimensional.

YOU WILL NEED

hinged wooden box

latex paint: turquoise and three pastel colors

paintbrushes

stencil cardboard and scalpel

4 plates

2 rollers

brown stamping ink and minibus stamp

one *Apply two coats of turquoise latex paint to the box. Cut out the background shape stencil. It should be large enough for the whole stamp.*

two *Spread the three pastel-colored paints on plates. Roll the first color through the stencil onto the box. You need a shape for each color. Wash the roller and apply the two remaining colors, painting through the stencil as before. Balance the shapes with an equal amount of background color. Let dry.*

three *Pour some brown ink onto a plate. Coat the rubber stamp with the ink using a rubber roller. Stamp the bus motif onto the pastel background patches.*

four *Let the stamps overlap the patches and vary the angle.*

BATHROOMS

MOST PEOPLE'S IDEA OF an imaginatively designed bathroom used to be stacking towels according to color and arranging three empty perfume bottles on the windowsill. Not anymore. Bathrooms have come of decorating age, and deservedly so.

Bathrooms are a refuge from the cares of the world, where you can soak and pamper yourself with unashamed self-indulgence. But to get a bathroom that you actually want to spend quality time in, first you must pamper your surroundings.

Cream, white and washed-out pastels are always popular, and for good reason—they make small areas look larger. But there's no need to adhere blindly to white. What about, for example, a beach look?

Brightly colored metal beach buckets hung from a piece of driftwood should do the trick. You could cover a wall with plaster stars or create a mosaic splashback of china. The view from the bath is looking better all the time.

What about views you don't want to see? Cover windows without losing light with blinds made of translucently colored woven scrim, or strips of parched wood from a broken-up orange crate—simple solutions that can be created in a matter of hours. And when night falls, turn off the cold overhead light and switch on a small lamp.

One idea to make your bathroom a bit unusual is to use bright buckets as containers. Buckets from the seaside will remind everyone of summer vacation.

Three chrome flashlights attached to a chrome rod to spotlight special items make a spectacular effect.

Relegate the plastic laundry basket to the kids' room, and in its place put an antique-finished terra-cotta pot. To step over, rather than into, puddles of water on the floor, lay strips of raised wooden duckboards. It's easy and very practical.

The ideas in this chapter provide a bathroom in which you can wash, shower, bathe and unwind. Whether you go for the bright beach look, the classical Roman touch or the crisp, cool serenity of Japanese style, there will be just one problem—once inside, you'll never want to leave!

BATHROOM BUCKETS

ADD AN ELEMENT OF seaside fun to your bathroom—as well as useful extra storage for all those odd-shaped items—by hanging up this row of bright buckets. This trio of enamel-painted buckets was bought at a toy store, but you could take a trip to the seaside where you are bound to find a great selection of buckets in all shapes and sizes. While there, go for a stroll along the shore to find the ideal pieces of driftwood to attach to your wall.

YOU WILL NEED

3 enamel-painted buckets
(or plastic seaside ones)
length of driftwood
(or an old plank)
pencil
drill, with wood and masonry bits
wire
pliers
wire cutters
masking tape
plastic anchors and screws
screwdriver

one *Line the buckets up at equal distances along the wood. Make two marks, one at each end of the handle where it dips, for the three buckets. Using the wood bit, drill through the six marked positions to make holes through the wood.*

two *Wind wire around each handle end and poke it through the holes. Twist the two ends together at the back to secure. Trim the ends. Then drill a hole near each end of the wood.*

three *Hold the piece of wood in place and mark the positions for the attachments. Place a small piece of masking tape over the tile to prevent it from cracking, then drill the holes and attach the wood to the wall.*

SEASHELL BOX

BOXES DECORATED WITH seashells can be ugly, and unfortunately the worst ones have given this wonderfully relaxing pastime a bad name. But don't be dismayed—shells are naturally beautiful and there are endless ways of arranging them tastefully. This project combines the contemporary look of corrugated cardboard with a dynamic shell arrangement. For the finishing touch, the box is painted pure white matte.

YOU WILL NEED

selection of seashells

round corrugated cardboard box with lid

glue gun with all-purpose glue sticks (or all-purpose glue)

white acrylic paint (gesso primer is ultra white)

paintbrush

one *Lay out all the shells and sort them into different shapes and sizes. Arrange them on the lid to make the design. Remove the top layer of shells from the middle of the lid and begin sticking them on. Heat the glue gun and glue the outside shells first, gradually moving inward.*

two *Work with the shell shapes, building up the middle section. The glue gun lets you get an instant bond, so the shells will stick to the surface however you want them to.*

three *Paint the box and the lid white. If you are using acrylic gesso primer, two coats will give a good matte covering. If you are using ordinary acrylic or latex, the box will benefit from an extra coat of paint.*

TERRA-COTTA LAUNDRY POT

LAUNDRY IN A FLOWERPOT? It certainly sounds unusual, but this idea makes a refreshing change from the ubiquitous wicker basket in the bathroom. Terra-cotta pots are now available in a huge range of shapes and sizes and a visit to your local garden center should provide you with just the right pot. To give a pristine pot an antique feel, follow these simple steps. This project would look good in a bathroom with a Mediterranean decor.

YOU WILL NEED

large terra-cotta flowerpot
rag
shellac button polish
white latex paint
paintbrushes
scouring pad
sandpaper (optional)

one *Soak a rag in button polish and rub all over the surface of the pot with it. The polish will sink in very fast, leaving a yellow sheen.*

two *Mix white latex paint with an equal quantity of water. Stir it thoroughly and apply a coat to the pot. Let the paint wash dry.*

three *Rub the pot with the scouring pad to remove most of the white paint. The paint will cling to the crevices and along the moldings to look like limescale. Either leave the pot like this or rub over it even more with sandpaper to reveal the clay. When you are happy with the effect, apply a coat of button polish with a brush to seal the surface.*

VICTORIAN STENCILING

THIS IDEA ORIGINATED from the etched glass windows of the Victorian era. You can easily achieve the frosted, etched look on plain glass by using a stencil cut from stencil cardboard and car enamel paint. The paint needs to be sprayed very lightly, so practice on some picture frame glass first to judge the effect. The stencil design is shown here, but you could easily design your own. Look at examples of lace panels to get some inspiration.

YOU WILL NEED

tape measure

masking tape

tracing paper

stencil cardboard

pencil

craft knife

brown paper

matte white car enamel spray

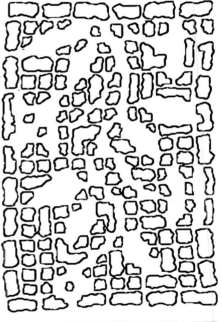

one *Measure the panes and mark the halfway points with masking tape. Photocopy and enlarge the stencil design and cut it from stencil cardboard. Tape the main stencil pattern in position, then use brown paper to mask off the surrounding area, at least 20 inches deep on all sides. (The spray spreads more than you would think.)*

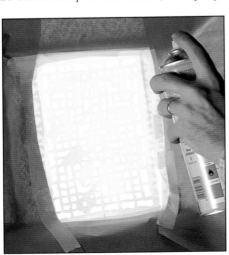

two *Shake the paint can thoroughly, as this affects the fineness of the spray. Spray from a distance of at least 12 inches, using short puffs of spray.*

three *Depending on the dimensions of the window panes, there may be strips along the sides of the main panel that also need stenciling. This pattern has a border to fit around the edge—you may need to adapt it to fit your pane.*

FLASHLIGHTS

A ROW OF ANGLED chrome spotlights adds the designer touch to any shelf display, but wiring and attaching them can be a time-consuming and expensive undertaking, especially with the extra safety factors essential in a bathroom. Here is a way to obtain an even better effect without spending a lot of money or even plugging anything into the electrical circuit. All you need is three cheap chrome flashlights, a length of towel rail with sockets, a few fixtures and an hour to spare.

YOU WILL NEED

3 small or medium chrome
flashlights

3 small leather straps

pencil

hole punch

3 small clips

chrome shower rail
with 2 sockets

screwdriver

drill, with masonry bit

plastic anchors and screws

level

one *Wrap a strap around a flashlight and mark the point where the buckle spike should enter. This will guarantee a good tight fit. Mark all the other straps in the same way.*

two *Punch a hole in each strap where marked. Slide the clips over the rail, loop a strap through each, then use a screwdriver to tighten the clips.*

three *Ensure that they are spaced evenly. Place the rail into the sockets and attach these to the wall. Use a level to ensure that the rail is straight before attaching. Buckle the flashlights to the rail.*

ORANGE CRATE BLIND

GREENGROCERS ARE ACCUSTOMED to supplying raw materials to their customers, but they might be a little surprised when you ask them for their wooden crates rather than their fruit and vegetables. Get some orange crates if you can, as the thin planks make ideal and original slats for blinds. These wooden blinds work best on a small, permanently obscurable window, such as in the bathroom. Although the blinds look Venetian, they don't actually pull up, but with a bit of perseverance you could probably make them do so. Here the wood was left natural, but it could be stained any color.

YOU WILL NEED

orange crates

pliers

sharp knife

medium- and fine-grade sandpaper

ruler

pencil

drill, and wood bit

string

scissors

2 cup hooks

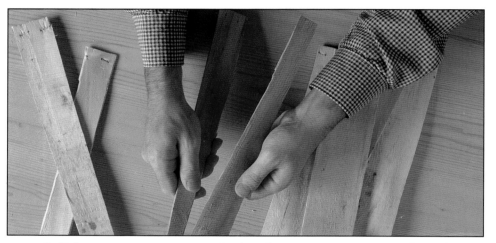

one *Pull the orange crates apart and select the most interesting parts from the longest sides. Remove any wire staples with pliers. Split some of the planks so that the slats are not all the same size. The final effect is more successful if the pieces are intentionally irregular.*

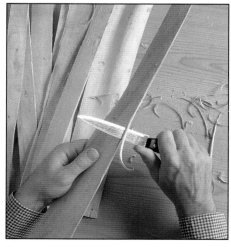

two *Shave off some of the wood to add character to the finished blind.*

three *Use medium-grade sandpaper first and then fine-grade sandpaper to smooth the wood and round off the edges.*

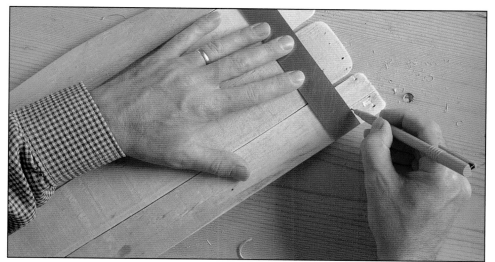

four *Place the slats side by side so that the edges line up. Mark a point 2 inches from each end and 1¼ inches from the bottom long edge. Although the slats are different widths, the holes should be drilled through points that line up on the front of the blind.*

five *Drill through the positions you have marked. The holes should be big enough to take the string through twice, but no bigger.*

six *Begin threading the string through the blind. Go through the blind from the back and pull a long length, about twice the drop of the window. It must be threaded all the way down the blind, to include all the looping around the slats.*

seven *Loop the string back over the slat and thread it through the hole a second time.*

◄
eight *Take the string up through the second slat. Continue as you did with the first, looping it around and through each slat twice, working all the way up the slats.*

CONTINUED OVER ➤

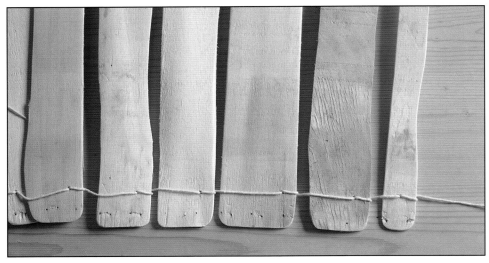

nine *When you get to the last slat, tie the string in a double knot and cut it off. Repeat this process on the other side. This is what the blind will look like from the "working side."*

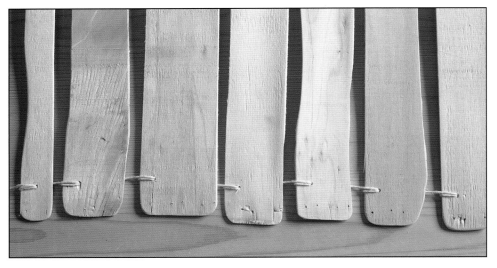

ten *Turn the blind around as shown to hang it up so that you only see the string entering and leaving each slat. Screw two hooks up into the window frame and hang up the blind.*

Mosaic Splashback

Mosaics look complicated and elaborate but are actually very simple to do; you just need time and patience to complete the job. Use broken tiles or look for chipped flea market finds to make a unique splashback for behind a sink. You can have as simple or as complicated a color scheme as you wish. You need a good selection of differently sized pieces. Break up the tiles, plates and so on by putting them between two pieces of cardboard and hammering them gently, but firmly. The cardboard will prevent tiny chips from flying around. Work on a piece of fiberboard so that you can sit down with the mosaic on a table, which is less back-breaking than applying the mosaic directly onto a wall.

YOU WILL NEED

tape measure

sheet of medium-density fiberboard

pencil

triangle or ruler

jigsaw

drill, with wood and masonry bits

beading

miter block and saw or miter saw

wood glue

white latex paint

paintbrush

selection of broken tiles and ceramic fragments

glue gun and glue sticks

screws

grout

plastic anchors

screwdriver

one *Measure the fiberboard to fit the width of your sink. Draw your chosen splashback shape onto the fiberboard using a pencil and a triangle or ruler.*

two *Carefully cut out the shape using a jigsaw.*

three *Mark the position of the holes that will be used to attach the splashback to the wall. Drill the holes.*

four *Measure the beading that will frame the fiberboard. Miter the beading using a miter block or miter saw.*

five *Glue the beading in place with wood glue, following the manufacturer's instructions.*

six *When the glue is dry, paint the whole splashback white. Let dry.*

seven *Arrange the ceramic pieces on the splashback. Experiment until you have created a pleasing pattern.*

eight *Glue the ceramic pieces in place using the glue gun.*

nine *Put screws into the screw holes, to prevent grout from getting into the holes. Grout over the mosaic, being careful near any raised, pointed bits.*

CONTINUED OVER ➤

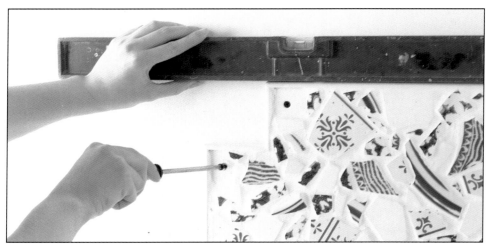

ten *Drill holes into the wall and insert the plastic anchors. Then screw the splashback into position onto the wall.*

eleven *Glue on more ceramic pieces, to hide the screws.*

twelve *Re-grout over these pieces.*

DECKING

THE JAPANESE BATHHOUSE is the inspiration for this floor treatment, preventing pools of water from turning your bathroom into a skating rink and, at the same time, imparting the serenity of a Zen garden. In this project the decking forms a pontoon or walkway across the bathroom, but you could also use sections and cut them around the bathroom furniture. Ready-made decking is also available in strips or squares.

YOU WILL NEED

tape measure

saw

quadrant beading

decking or duckboards

drill, with wood bit and pilot bit

soft cloth

paintbrush

wood stain

wood screws

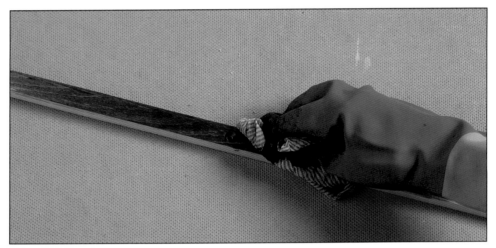

one *Make sure you have a clean, level floor: cork tiles, wood and linoleum are all suitable. The existing floor will show through, so if you want to change the color, do so now. Measure and cut the two lengths of beading to the same length as the runners on the decking or duckboards. Drill holes through these new runners. Stain the two new long runners to the same color as the decking or duckboards.*

two *Measure the distance between the runners on the decking or duckboards.*

three *Space the new runners at a distance that will let the decking or duckboard runners slide between them, holding the board steady but letting it be lifted up for cleaning. Screw in place by drilling through the subfloor, using the correct type of bit for the type of floor you have. Slide the boards into place.*

PATCHWORK EFFECT TILES

BATHROOMS AND SHOWER ROOMS are often thought of simply as basic utility rooms because they tend to get heavily splashed and also, with today's busy lifestyle, most people spend little time there. Consequently, their floorings are frequently correspondingly spartan. However, the wide range of ceramic tiles now available enables you to achieve stunning good looks without sacrificing practicality. Here we opted for stylish blue tiles in the same color range, accented by deep indigo.

YOU WILL NEED

pencil

ruler

tile adhesive (waterproof for bathrooms; flexible if on a suspended floor)

ceramic tiles

notched spreader

tile spacers

straightedge (optional)

squeegee

grout

damp sponge

lint-free dry cloth

dowel scrap

one *Draw a grid on the floor for the tiles. Using the spreader, spread some adhesive on an area of the floor small enough to be reached easily. Start laying the tiles. As you do so, use spacers to ensure that the gaps between them are even. Use a straightedge to check that all the tiles are horizontal and level. When all the tiles have been laid, use a squeegee to spread grout over them and fill all the seams—this is for both appearance and waterproofing.*

two *Wipe off the surplus grout with a damp sponge before it dries.*

three *Buff with a dry cloth when the grout has hardened, then smooth the grout with the scrap piece of dowel.*

Woven Blind

THIS COLORED MESH RIBBON is one of the new natural materials now available. It is stiff enough to hold its shape and be folded into sharp creases to make a blind. Use this treatment for a window that must be obscured from prying eyes while still allowing maximum light to penetrate the room—a bathroom, shower room or toilet. To make the most of their interesting texture and soft colors, the ribbons have been interwoven.

YOU WILL NEED

strips of woven mesh ribbon in 3 colors, 2½ inches wide

scissors

tape measure

2 broom handles

staple gun

awl

2 plumbers' pipe attachments

screwdriver

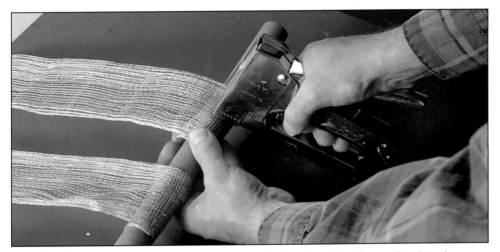

one *Cut lengths of woven mesh ribbon to the length of the drop, plus 8 inches. Wrap a 4-inch length around a broom handle and secure it with a staple gun. Leaving 1¼-inch gaps between each ribbon, continue attaching the ribbons along the broom handle with the staple gun. Finish with 3½ inches of bare wood at the end. Repeat this process to attach the ends of the strips to the second broom handle.*

two *Cut the remaining two colors into strips to fit the width of the blind, plus a 1¼-inch allowance on each side. Weave these through the first ribbons.*

three *At each side, turn the seam over and crease it with your thumbnail, then staple the two ribbons together. Use an awl to make two small holes on either side of the underside of the top recess, then screw in the plumbers' fittings. Put the broom handle in position, then screw the front section of the fittings into position.*

HAND-PRINTED "TILES"

THESE IMITATION TILES ARE, in fact, hand-printed onto the wall using a homemade foam stamp. This is a quicker and less expensive alternative to ceramic tiles, and there are endless color combinations. If you opt for shades of one color, it is inexpensive because you can buy one pot of paint and lighten it with white to achieve different shades. Making a sponge stamp to apply the color is a quick and foolproof way of getting squares of color onto the wall. If you start with a white wall, the lines left between the fake tiles will look like the grouting between real tiles.

YOU WILL NEED
ruler
pencil
scrap paper
high-density foam
glue
craft knife
self-healing cutting mat
latex paint in 2 colors, plus white
paintbrushes
scissors
straightedge
level
old plates
small roller
small brush
clear varnish
varnish brush

one *Decide on the size of the tiles. Draw your design for the stamp on paper. Glue it to the foam and cut out unwanted areas. Angle the cut outward slightly from top to bottom. Make a stamp for each color. For this design you need six stamps.*

two *Use smaller pieces of foam to make a handle on the back of each stamp.*

three *Choose your colors—aquatic greens and blues work well in bathrooms. Here, a scheme of six shades, made from two basic colors, was used. One-third of each color was mixed together to make a third color, and then these three colors were halved again and lightened with white.*

four *Decide on the pattern; small-scale paper squares, painted in the different colors and/or shades, will help you plan the design.*

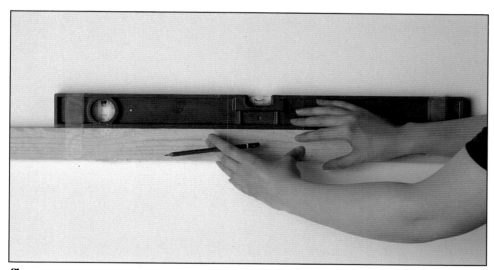

five *Mark horizontal guidelines on the wall with faint pencil lines, using a straightedge and a level.*

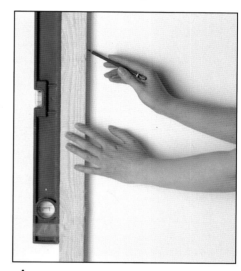

six *Mark vertical guidelines in the same way.*

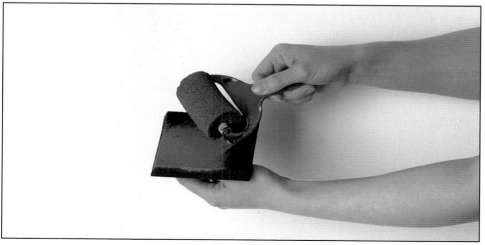

seven *Put some paint onto a plate and run the roller through it until it is evenly coated, then roll the paint onto the first stamp.*

CONTINUED OVER ➤

eight *Stamp the "tile" pattern onto the wall, pressing down firmly with your fingers. Go around the "grout" area and touch up any smudges with white paint and a small brush. Make sure no pencil guidelines are visible.*

nine *When dry, apply two coats of varnish to protect the surface and give it a wipeable finish.*

PLASTER STARS

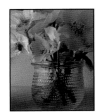

PLASTER HAS A POWDERY quality and a pure white color, which make it an especially interesting wall embellishment. Also, of course, it can be painted in any color of your choice. Most decorative plaster firms have lots of simple shapes—both modern and traditional—to choose from and will make a mold of virtually anything you like, so the possible variations of this effect are endless. This idea works well as a border above a skirting board or around a door, as well as in a defined area, such as behind a sink, as shown here.

YOU WILL NEED

plaster stars
scissors
masking tape
white glue or clear varnish
paintbrush
wall adhesive
wood scrap

one *Decide on the design and spacing of the stars (or the fancy plaster motifs of your choice) by making photocopies of them, cutting them out and using small pieces of masking tape to attach them to the wall. Try out a number of versions until you are happy with the final effect.*

two *Seal the stars with clear varnish or white glue mixed with water.*

three *When the stars are dry, use wall adhesive to attach them to the walls. Use a wood scrap as a spacer for positioning the stars on the wall.*

GREEK KEY BATHROOM

This bathroom looks far too stylish to have been decorated by an amateur. The border design is a classic Greek key interspaced with a bold square and a cross. The black and gold look stunning on a pure white tiled wall. Every bathroom has different features, so use the border to make the most of the best ones, while drawing attention away from the duller areas. If you want a coordinated scheme, you could print a border on a set of towels, using fabric inks.

YOU WILL NEED

tracing paper

pencil

spray adhesive

high-density foam, such as upholstery foam

scalpel

acrylic enamel paint: black and gold

2 plates

length of wood, 3/4-1 1/4 inches wide, depending on the bathroom

masking tape

one *Trace and transfer the pattern shapes from the template. Lightly spray the shapes with adhesive and place them on the foam. To cut out the shapes, cut the outline first, then undercut and remove any excess, leaving the pattern shape standing free from the foam.*

two *Apply an even coating of black paint onto a plate. Place the length of wood up next to the door frame to keep the border an even distance from it. Make a test print on scrap paper, then begin by stamping one black outline square in the bottom corner, at chair-rail height. Print a key shape above it, being careful not to smudge the adjoining edge of the previous print.* ➤

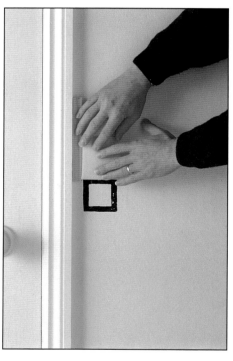

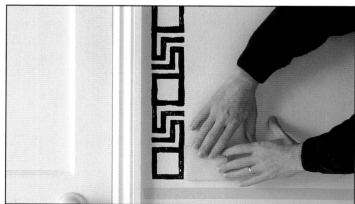

three *Continue alternating the stamps around the door. Mark the base line at chair-rail height with masking tape and alternate the designs along this line.*

four *Place a coating of gold paint onto a plate and dip the cross shape into it. Make a test print on scrap paper, then print the shape in the square frames.*

Math montage page 76

Country-style shelf page 94

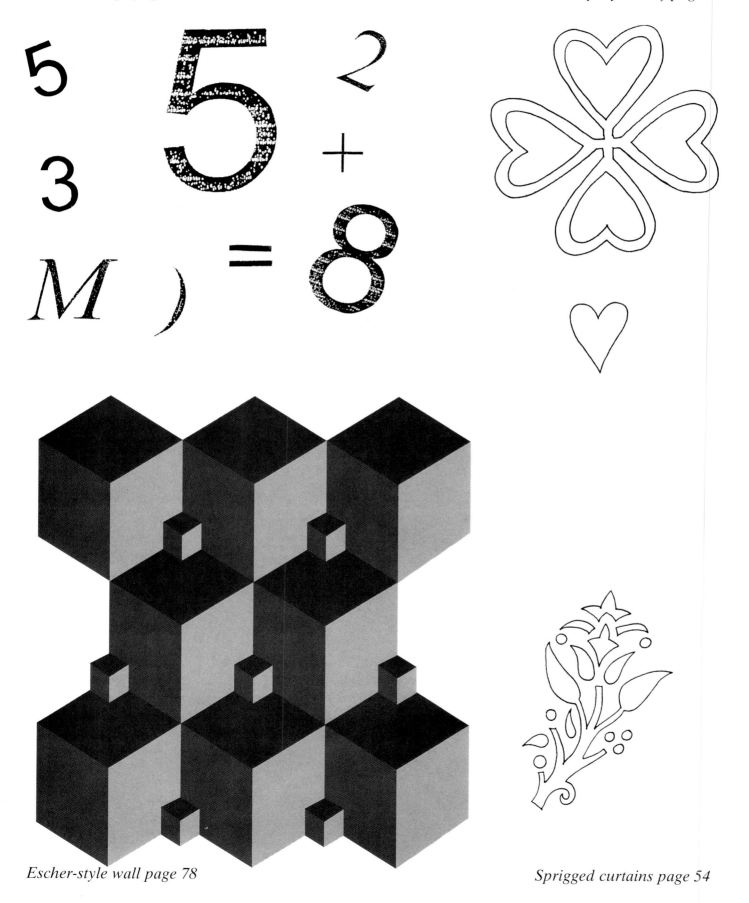

Escher-style wall page 78

Sprigged curtains page 54

Draped director's chair page 36

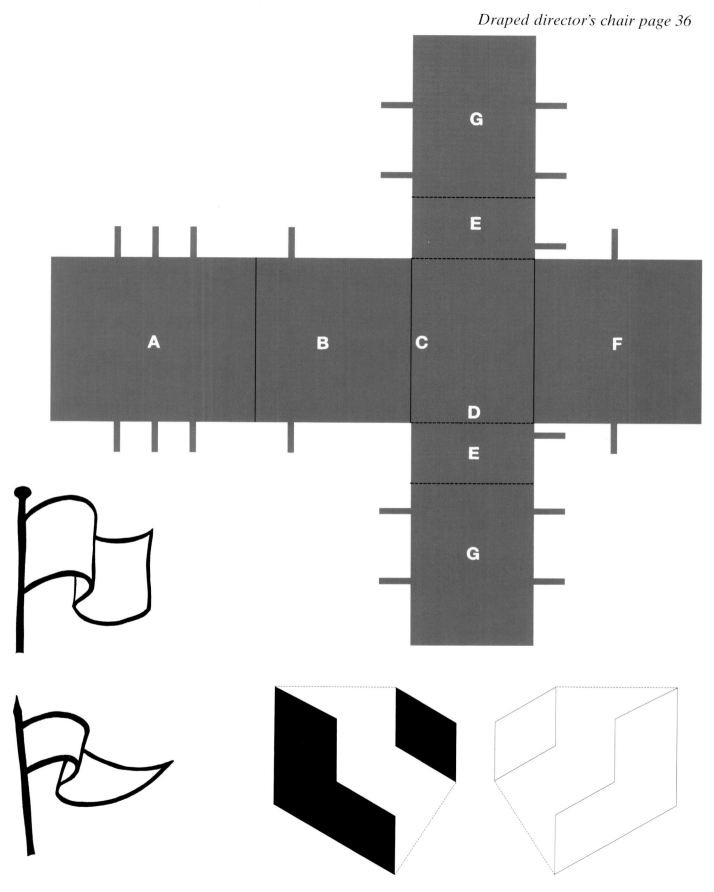

G

E

D

E

A   B   C   F

G

Flag stencils page 194

Escher's deckchair page 80

Trompe-l'oeil linoleum page 112

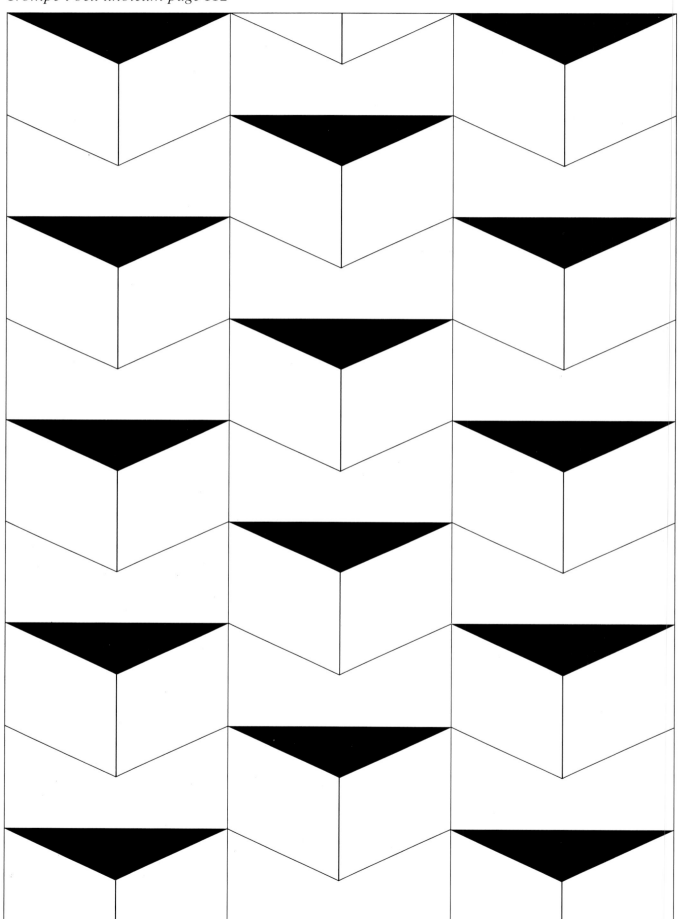

Vermeer-style marble page 114

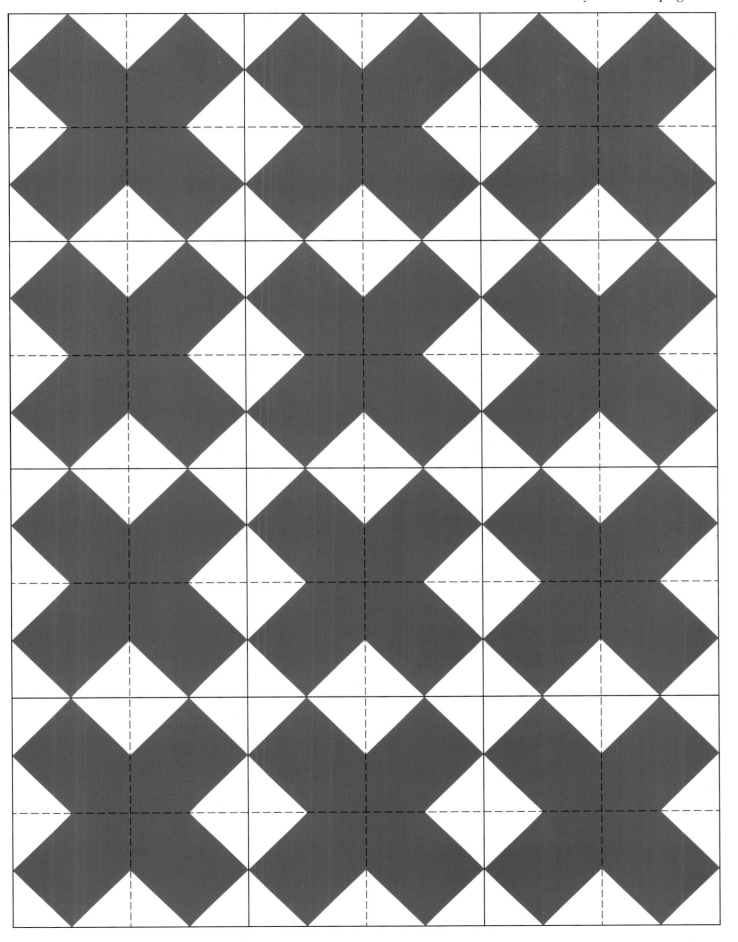

INDEX